THE
SEARCH
FOR
XAVIER

SEAN WALSH

"Fugitivus. Once a dull word in a dry textbook.
Now it - it's screaming at me..."

DEDICATION. IN FRATERNITATE...

Paris. Circa 2010. In a bistro near Notre Dame, Jim and I meet up: pasta, wine, coffee - and talk, talk!.. And when I mentioned - shyly, reluctantly - an idea for a drama that was, as yet, very much in embryo his eyes lit up and he became an instant fan! Then questions, questions! And in striving to formulate answers the project began to crystallize in my mind...

Fast forward to 2012. Act One of The Reckoning, a stage play in two acts, written, edited, printed... a copy posted as an email attachment to Paris. His reaction was quite spontaneous:

"What can I say?.. What can I say!.. Riveting!.. Absolutely riveting!.. so pleased and excited about what you are doing. You certainly have this play in you and it just needs to come out. I love the dialogue. The characterisation is authentic and varied. You create and hold the dramatic intensity... Delighted, really delighted..."

Fast forward to 2014. Despite such an enthusiastic endorsement, I lingered, dithered, procrastinated... Then, finally, I began to write again - and in earnest. Gradually Act Two materialized. And a second email to Paris with attachment. (Between times I had changed the title while still unsure about the actual format: stage, video, audio?..) Back came Jim's response:

"What a play! What a play! What would it be like to see it!.. You have done a super job. Bless you. There are the amusing bits. Its great fun. But then it fills me with sadness. It makes me cross. It makes me mad. I want to cry. I'm enveloped in the world that was yesterday... witness a personal tragedy unfold in the twilight of that evening then itself fading."

I gratefully dedicate this publication to a great friend, a dear companion of Yesteryear, an unwavering enthusiast without whose strong support it might never have come to pass: *James Hynes.*

STORY LINE

An insider piece: set in a friary/priory in Dublin, Ireland, in the late 60's.

A play centred on a community of friars in the immediate aftermath of Vatican Two but before the effects of that Council have really begun to take effect... Inside the cloister, behind closed doors.

The status quo is shaken when one of the brethren disappears overnight; a young priest goes AWL...

Worry... speculation... finally, consternation: the search for Xavier ends when it is established beyond doubt that he is in London and co-habiting with a female...

A search that gives rise, in turn, to a searching of hearts...

Why the 60's?

A modern audience will be able to look back/look into the Church as it was at that time;

the strict regime of "the old days" had only just begun to give way to the changes and uncertainties resulting from Vatican Two;

the old regime of "black is black - white, white" was slowly, inexorably, being eroded;

the element of fear - correction, reprimand, punishment, transfer - loomed large in the clerical psyche;

the shock waves caused by the defection of Charles Davis from the priesthood and the diocese of Westminster had only just begun to reverberate around the universal Church;

the old certainties had begun to give way to the new uncertainties;

when the term, paedophile, was far from common coinage;

when the debate on clerical celibacy/married clergy was still in its infancy;

when the aristocratic Pope Pius XII was still a vivid memory in the minds of the faithful;

when the clerics and religious who lived at that time could not have foreseen the scandals that would rock the Church of the 80's and subsequent decades...

Briefly, a modern audience will be able to look back at the Church of the 60's - a Church that no longer exists to any great extent - an era that formed their forebears; view it objectively and with a certain curiosity.

A Church of Change - of friction, dispute, challenge, doubt, uncertainty, the old absolutes gone for ever.

There are several orders of friars/male religious in the Church: Dominicans, Franciscans, Augustinians, Carmelites etc. Each with its own insignia, rule. Variations on a theme.

The Latin of the liturgy - Mass, Divine Office - is contrasted betimes with the music, laughter and bonhomie of a community at recreation.

The song - *Mary Anne* - is a piece of nostalgia that was well known among the friars at that time. The chorus rouses them to join in… at the centre and again at the end… rising to crescendo… before giving way to moriendo…

For words and music score in full, vide Addendum.

THE SET.

Inside the priory/friary:

The action/storyline moves from one area to another - but nearly always within the friary:

sacristy

choir

kitchen

recreation room

Xavier's room

Provincial's office

library

Mass office

Rector's office

tailory

Church, high altar

CAST

The Priests

MARK :
The Prior of the Community i.e., Rector/local Superior. Late 40's/early 50's. Ebullient, out-going... A good Churchman... Well organised and a good organiser... Has a short fuse, at times, in dealing with some of his charges. Under pressure - debts, bills, complaints - and tends to cultivate favourites among the brethren to the partial exclusion of others...

HUGO:
Middle-aged. A middle-of-the-road man. Never puts a foot wrong. Enjoys the good things in life - the permitted ones, that is: golf, a G and T, the glass of wine, the bit of travel... Plays his cards close to his chest, would never take a chance, go out on a limb... Keeps in with the powers that be...

FINTAN:
In his 50's. Well read, well spoken. Something of an intellectual and quite a political animal. Is consulted by the Prior because of his expertise in Canon Law... Thus he is somewhat smug in the security of his tenure as a member of the Community. An active Churchman...

EMMANUEL:
Old, rather senile. Long since retired as a Professor of Church History, he tends to live in the past for the most part. Needs constant minding. A stammerer, prone to spoonerisms. Can be quite sarcastic, betimes. Petulant. Weak, high-pitched voice...

JUSTIN:
About 36. Just home, having completed his second stint in South Africa as a missionary. Tanned, energetic, out-going... A no-nonsense man's man... The petty rules and regulations of Community life now tend to bug him. Functions as catalyst in the confrontational scenes...

AIDAN:

In his late 20's. Still an idealist, he is quite removed from the hard-boiled pragmatism of the older priests... Something of a dreamer and more than something of a poet. Literature is his second love. Nervous, emotional. In awe of authority and yet ready to revolt at what he sees as status quo mediocrity. Teaches full-time in a school in the inner (deprived) City...

GILES:

Late 50's, early 60's. If ever there was a settled bachelor... Over-fed, over-slept, over-weight... Quite unaware that he is a caricature. High pitched voice, a whiner, constantly complaining... Does the minimum amount of work, keeps harping back to the days when he himself was a local Superior... And yet for all that, there is a streak of real humanity in him which surfaces as the Drama evolves...

JARLATH:

The Minister Provincial. A minor player. 2/3 scenes. In his 50's. Bearing the burden of office none too lightly. Beset by problems, nation wide. Plays strictly according to the book.

The Brothers

SENAN

A wee jovial tub of a man from the South of Ireland. Has the gift of the gab, would charm the birds off the trees. In his 60's. Not a great cook but a deft hand at "stirring it..." An expert at chatting up priests and Superiors. Always makes sure to keep on the right side of the Prior.

GEORGE

Ex-Army. Still somewhat rigid in his actions, walk, stance, attitudes. A stickler for discipline, rules and regulations. Originally from Northern Ireland. Views Catholicism as practised in the South with a certain disdain. In his 50's. The Community tailor.

DECLAN

Old, rural, loving, lovable, frail, soft-spoken, a man of prayer and peace.
The Sacristan, he looks after the altars, lights, candles, vestments, etc. A
taker of snuff, he is quite unaware of the stains on his habit or anything to
do with his personal appearance... The changes in the Church being
brought about by Vatican Two have unsettled him. Seldom ventures
outside the Cloister. Shy in the presence of women.

JOHN

50-ish. Big, tall, ascetic, a man of prayer, few words. Deep voice, musical.
The Refectorian, he also doubles as the Community Infirmarian - though
he has no training as a nurse. His primary function, then, is to look after -
and to look out for - the ageing Emmanuel, a task that would try the
patience of a saint...

Extras. Non speaking parts... As in Epilogue... choir scenes... community
recreation scenes... refectory... etc. Male singers dressed as friars especially
important for a stirring rendition of *"Dies Ira, Dies Irae"* when friars carry
Emmanuel's coffin shoulder high from the back of the church down
through the congregation and up unto the Sanctuary, High Altar, at the
beginning of Part Two. (pg. 112)

E P I L O G U E

THE REFECTORY:

FRIARS ENTER... GROUP, FORM...
OLD, MIDDLE-AGED, YOUNG... LEAN, STOUT, TALL, SMALL...
NERVOUS, APPREHENSIVE... MIME WHISPERED
CONVERSATION...

THEY BREAK OFF AS A BELL RINGS, OFF.

THE MINISTER PROVINCIAL ENTERS, WEARING A SURPLICE
AND STOLE OVER HIS HABIT, HOLDING A BOOK/RITUAL.
HE STANDS, CENTRE...

JARLETH   'No joy... 'Gives me no joy...

HE OPENS THE RITUAL... READS:

In accordance with the rules of Canon Law
and the constitution of our Holy Rule...
I, Jarlath, Minister Provincial by the will of God,
do solemnly hereby declare...

that our erstwhile brother, Father Xavier,
having taken flight with a female,
and showing no sign of remorse or contrition -

the calendar month since his departure
from the cloister without permission
having now expired -

to be excloistrated... and excommunicated.

HE CLOSES THE RITUAL. SOME OF THE FRIARS MAKE A HALF-
HEARTED ATTEMPT AT THE SIGN OF THE CROSS... SHUFFLE...

Eh-hh... Tomorrow morning... eleven o'clock... the High
Altar... I will offer Mass for Xavier... that God may bless
and guide him in his new way of life...

I invite all of you who may be free to join me...

HE TURNS AWAY, EXITS, AS THE FRIARS TURN BACK INTO
SMALL GROUPS, BEGIN TO MIME INTENSE CONVERSATION...

ACT ONE

SCENE 1   **THE SACRISTY**.

DECLAN STANDS AT A WALL PHONE, RECEIVER TO HIS EAR.
JOHN APPROACHES.

JOHN   Good morning, Declan.

DECLAN   Ah... John...

DECLAN REPLACES THE RECEIVER

JOHN   I'll tell you, that was some wind last night.

DECLAN   'Not like him at all...

JOHN   I didn't get off for. . . 'Anything wrong, Brother?

DECLAN   Ah, it's just... I'm after ringing up to Father Xavier. He's
              down for the seven Mass, like.

JOHN   No answer?.. Hmmm... He could be up before the time - a
              broken sleep, maybe - 'gone round to the showers? Or the
              loo?..

DECLAN   You'd think he'd ring down, let me know?..

JOHN   Best go up in the lift, so. I can look after here?

DECLAN   'Never know, you never know...

JOHN	Ah, come on now, Declan! 'Tis a sapling you're rousing, not an old oak. Now if it was poor Father Emmanuel and him going out of himself every day that passes?..
DECLAN	(GOING) Aye... I suppose...
JOHN	Would you like me to go, Brother, you stay put?..
DECLAN	Yerra, no... Just you say the prayer, Brother John...

SCENE 2   THE CHOIR

THE BRETHREN IN CHOIR, RECITING THE DIVINE OFFICE. LATIN. A "NOT EASY ON THE EAR" SOUND, THIS.

TEN TO FIFTEEN MEN - SOME OF THEM STILL TIRED AFTER AN EARLY RISE - CHANTING IN MONOTONE, SOME QUICKER THAN OTHERS... DEFINITELY NOT GREGORIAN CHANT AT ITS BEST... RATHER RAGGED...

DECLAN QUICKLY ENTERS... GENUFLECTS... CROSSES TO MARK, WHISPERS IN HIS EAR. MARK NODS... THEY BOTH EXEUNT.

SCENE 3   **THE CORRIDOR** OUTSIDE THE CHOIR…

THE CHANTING FADES TO BACKGROUND.

MARK   Yes, Declan?

DECLAN   I'm sorry for calling you out, Father -

MARK   What is it, Brother?

DECLAN   Well, like, Father Xavier's down for to say the seven.

MARK   I'm aware of that.

DECLAN   It's just, when I went to call him - well, he's not in his room.

MARK   Oh?

DECLAN   'No answer when I rang him on the house phone. And when I went up, thinkin' mebbe he was in a heavy sleep or, or even up before the time –

MARK   Get to the point, Brother - please.

DECLAN   His bed's not slept in, Father.

MARK   Hmmm. And no sign of him?

DECLAN   None.

MARK   Did you look around? The Library? Community Room?

DECLAN   Empty.

MARK   All right, then. I'll stand in for him on the High Altar -

DECLAN   I'll dress your chalice and -

MARK   So now we have a sleep-walker in the Community.

DECLAN   Well, and if we have, Father Prior, is it in the nude or what he's in, I'm wonderin'?..

MARK: How do you mean?

DECLAN   His habit, Father. Xavier's habit is hanging up on the back of his door…

SCENE 4   THE SACRISTY

BROTHER JOHN KNEELING ON A PREDELLA…

HUGO	'Not many for confession… hardly a handful in the Church…
JOHN	(STANDING UP) Oh… Father Hugo…
HUGO	The weather that's in it… You wouldn't put out a milk bottle…

HE TURNS TO THE VESTMENTS LAID OUT ON THE COUNTER…

	'Jusr slip out to Saint Joseph's altar...
JOHN	Father, no. There's a change -
HUGO	What?
JOHN	The Prior says you're to hold on, say the eight on the High Altar.
HUGO	Oh?
JOHN	Father Xavier is… is -
HUGO	Where?
JOHN	Well, we don't know for sure, Father. 'Not in his room when Brother Declan went up to -
HUGO	Clown… What'll he get up to next?
JOHN	'Just saying a prayer for him, Father, that he'll be all -
HUGO	Oh, you don't worry yourself on that score, Brother. He'll be all right, no fear. A dab hand at looking after himself, the same Xavier… (GOING) I'll get a coffee while I'm waiting... have a fag...

SCENE 5   THE KITCHEN.

A JOVIAL BROTHER SENAN BUSY WITH POTS, PANS, KETTLE COMING TO THE BOIL, ETC... SINGING TO HIMSELF A BROKEN SNATCH OF *MARY ANNE*...

"Put more turf on the fire, Mary Anne...for the weather is..."

HUGO APPROACHES...

SENAN	Ah, Father Hugo - is it yourself?
HUGO	Just about...
SENAN	'Sausages in the top oven - or would you like me to do you a rasher and egg?
HUGO	No thanks... just coffee...
SENAN	And the fag. A fallen woman's breakfast! Ha, ha, ha!
HUGO	Spare me, Senan. I'm a bit fragile...
SENAN	Oh-hh?.. Rough night, was it?..
HUGO	Ah-hh... Two or three of us stayed on at the end of Recreation, 'got stuck in...
SENAN	Say no more!.. Whiskey's the divil! That last case the Prior got in, sure God, man, you wouldn't use it to take paint off a door - 'might damage the woodwork!.. Ha, ha, ha!
HUGO	Easy... Easy, Senan...
SENAN	(SUBSIDING) Yerra, I know how you feel - only too well...
HUGO	So... What's the story?
SENAN	What?

15

HUGO	Where is he?
SENAN	Huh?
HUGO	Xavier.
SENAN	'Cross me heart, Father, you know as much as I do, more mebbe. Brother Declan it was whispered in me ear when I was coming down from the Choir... He - he wasn't at Recreation last night.
HUGO	Last night was optional. He could have been in his room...
SENAN	Hmmm... What do you reckon yourself, Father?
HUGO	Ah, out with friends. One too many, mebbe a skinful.
SENAN	I suppose, yeah. He's very popular, the same Xavier.
HUGO	They'd have put him up for the night, what else? Mark my words, Senan, a few hours from now he'll sail in, fresh as a daisy, and the rest of us fallin' off our feet with the sleep!..
SENAN	I wouldn't like to be in his sandals.
HUGO	Oh, he'll get away with it! A smile, the soft word in the Prior's ear and he'll be back in the good books again! Now if it was me -
DECLAN	(ENTERING, BREATHLESS) 'Just back from the garage, neither of the cars missing -
SENAN	So, we know he wasn't drivin'. That atself...

HUGO CHECKS HIS WATCH, LEAVES IN A HURRY.

SENAN	'Have to make a move. The Prior'll be in any minute -
DECLAN	No.
SENAN	What?

DECLAN	He won't. 'Asked Father Cathaldus to hear confessions for him during the eight and straight up the back stairs to Father Xavier's room.
SENAN	Oh?..
DECLAN	And here, here's one for you! He rang Father Fintan from the sacristy, told him to meet him there.
SENAN	Roused him, huh? God, Fintan won't like that - he's on the twelve.
DECLAN	The way the Prior spoke, I'd say he was up and dressed in jig time.
SENAN	Do y'tell me?.. 'Taking it very serious, so?
DECLAN	I've never seen him so uptight.
SENAN	Yerra, I don't know what all the ri-ra is about. Father Hugo was saying he mebbe had a sup too many out visiting -
DECLAN	Ah, no. No, Brother Senan. There's more to it than that.
SENAN	Huh? How do y'mean?
DECLAN	Well, you tell me: which of us in his right mind would go out and leave his only good habit hanging up in his room?
SENAN	Wha'?.. You mean?.. Ah, Jesus!
DECLAN	Amen.
SENAN	No! Oh, no…
DECLAN	Please God, no.
SENAN	No... 'Can't be... No!
DECLAN	All we can do now is say the prayer.
SENAN	(CROSSING HIMSELF)
	Jesus, Mary and Holy Saint Joseph...

SCENE 6   XAVIER'S ROOM.

MARK ALONE... PONDERING... ENTER FINTAN.

FINTAN	I just slipped on a dressing gown -
MARK	Close it.
FINTAN	(CLOSING DOOR) 'Nipped into the Oratory on the way up to get the oils - just in case -
MARK	If he was dead or dying I'd know what to do, Fintan. You'd still be asleep.
FINTAN	Well... then?
MARK	Have a look - the bed, behind the door...
FINTAN	Oh-hh... Oh, oh... Xavier?
MARK	(DRILY) This is his room...
FINTAN	Sorry. Of course, yes... Wardrobe... drawers, locker - empty...
MARK	Hmmm. Ten out of ten, Fintan... The other wall press is the same...
FINTAN	Christ Almighty!
MARK	If that was a prayer, let it be the first of many.
FINTAN	Sorry. Sorry, Father... Eh - up above, his suitcase, holdall?
MARK	Gone.
FINTAN	Oh, dear. Dear, dear, dear... A message, letter?
MARK	Nothing. I've looked around... 'Desk cleared.
FINTAN	'Last time I saw it, it was a mess... So you think?..
MARK	I don't rightly know what to think, Fintan. 'First time I've come up against - anything like this... At least now you know why I woke you. You're the expert in Canon Law: you tell me.

FINTAN	Hmmmm?
MARK	Where do we go from here?
FINTAN	Well... For a start, I think you should put your foot on it.
MARK	If I could!.. It's doing the rounds. Declan was the first, then Senan. John and Hugo will have it by now -
FINTAN	They'll all know in jig time.
MARK	But won't know what we know.
FINTAN	'Better lock the door. Key, is there a master key?
MARK	No such animal that I know of...
FINTAN	And no sign of his own bunch?
MARK	No. But there's this... 'Always kept it in this leather purse, never went on a sick call - or parlour duty - without it.
FINTAN	What?
MARK	'Given him when he was ordained in Rome. A relic of the true Cross...
FINTAN	Well, if he left that behind, he was really cutting himself off.
MARK	Hmmm… Have a think, Father. See what it says in the Code...
FINTAN	'Need to check a few - 'bout an hour? -
MARK	Fair enough. My Office… And I'll be more than interested in what the commentaries have to say...
FINTAN	Fugitivus...
MARK	Yeah. Fugitive... 'Just a dull word in a dry text-book... Now it - it's screaming at me...

SCENE 7   EMMANUEL'S ROOM.

JOHN ENTERS... CHECKS THE BED... PLACES TRAY ON
BEDSIDE LOCKER.

JOHN	Father?.. Father Emmanuel?..
MANUEL	Wh-what?
JOHN	Good morning, Father... Emmanuel?.. Good morrn -
MANUEL	Where? Where am I?
JOHN	It's all right, Father, it's only meself.
MANUEL	What? Who?
JOHN	Me, Father. That looks after you. Brother John. Sure don't you know me well?
MANUEL	Jo - John?
JOHN	I've brought you up your cup of tea, same as always.
EMMANUEL	Oh?.. Oh-hh..
JOHN	If you can just manage the tray...
MANUEL	What? Train? What train? To Louvain?
JOHN	No. No train, Father. And no Louvain. You're right here in Dublin in your own Community.
MANUEL	Late? Am I late? Lecture. Am I late for -
JOHN	Schhhush now, schhush. No lectures, no more. Will you try and sit up or you'll spill it for sure...
MANUEL	My notes! Where - where did I put my notes?..
JOHN	Come on now, try. I'll prop up your pillows. U-u-u-upppp we come!

JOHN'S EXERTION...

That's it, that's better... Now... won't you put your teeth in like a good man?.. Here we are...

GLASS TUMBLER... CLINKING... JOHN MANIPULATES THE DENTURES.

MANUEL	What? Why are you - ?
JOHN	Now! Now you can look the world in the eye... Hold still, Father, and I'll put the tray on your lap... Good strong drop it is... 'bring you back to yourself.
JOHN	(POURING, STIRRING) And the milk...
MANUEL	What - what time is it? Why are you calling me... middle of the night? What?
JOHN	Sure, we're well into the morning, Father. Here, I'll...

JOHN CROSSES TO THE WINDOW, RELEASES THE BLIND

Now! See?.. A grey day but there it is. Nothing I can do about it...

HE TURNS BACK TO THE BED... CUP, SAUCER...

Oh, watch it, Father dear, won't you..?

MANUEL	What? Watch who? Where - where are they?
JOHN	Just keep an eye on your cup like a good man. Good, that's good... And won't you eat the few pieces of toast? Brother Senan put honey on them, specially.
MANUEL	Money? What, what money? I haven't any money!
JOHN	Honey, Father Emmanuel. (LOUDER) Honey!

MANUEL	What? Why - why are you calling me honey? Who are you? What!
JOHN	Ah, God love you anyhow, you creathur!
MANUEL	What are you doing in my room? What!
JOHN	All right, all right, I'm going... I'll be just outside on the corridor if you need me. .. (REMEMBERING) Oh, aye. Did you use your pot during the night?.. Wait till we see now...

JOHN CHECKS CHAMBER POT

Ah, you did, you did! And didn't spill a drop. Aren't you the great man all the same?.. You are, you are, surely!.. I'll just go and empty it... Now where's the cloth?.. Ah, yeah.

JOHN COVERS THE POT WITH A CLOTH/HAND TOWEL

MANUEL	My - my family...
JOHN	What's that, Father?
MANUEL	My family were O-O-O Donnells on my m-m-mother's side - did you know?
JOHN	(HUMOURING HIM) No - never! Is that a fact now?
MANUEL	'Trace - can trace it b-back to the F-F-Flight of the Earls.
JOHN	Do y'tell me so? Well, isn't that remarkable? Remarkable, entirely...
MANUEL	The Wild Geese, you know... Wild Geese...
JOHN	Well, there's a wonder for you... And no doubt...

JOHN TURNS AWAY...

'Come to that?.. Oh, dear, dear. Brilliant, I'm told he was, only brilliant... All confusion now... facts and dates and...

No need to shave him. Tomorrow. Tomorrow will do. Every second day...

The Wild Geese... Dear, dear... The Flight of the... Dear, oh dear...

SCENE 8   THE TAILORY.

BROTHER GEORGE AT SEWING MACHINE... HE LOOKS UP AS AN AGITATED SENAN HURRIES IN.

SENAN   George! Do you know what I'm going to tell you?
GEORGE   I know.
SENAN   Wh-what?
GEORGE   Shut the door like a good man.
SENAN   Huh? Oh, yeah... (CLOSES DOOR)
GEORGE   'Bad enough in here without being in a draught. Brother
            Paul's threatening to fix yon window sash for the past
            month.
SENAN   Right, right... Well?
GEORGE   Well, what?

SENAN	George, I'm only over from the kitchen for a minute!
GEORGE	And I have to have this job ready by eleven. Father Bonaventure is flying out at -
SENAN	And what time would you say Xavier took off at?
GEORGE	Oh-hh. I reckon, when all honest men were sleeping in their beds.
SENAN	Ah, so you know!
GEORGE	I served Father Hugo's Mass.
SENAN	Ah, enough said.
GEORGE	'Funny...
SENAN	Huh?
GEORGE	It takes the central heating half the morning to get round this far - but a wee rumour, there's no stopping it...
SENAN	You never said a word to me when you came in for your breakfast?..
GEORGE	Nor to anyone else. Now if you don't mind -
SENAN	His suit, Brother George! Xavier's suit!
GEORGE	What about it?
SENAN	His blacks - that he had for going to England and up the North, missions and retreats..?
GEORGE	Oh-hh... I'll show you, Senan. I did a bit of mending for him just a few weeks ago.
SENAN	There y'see! It's not as bad as we feared: he's gone off in his blacks, for God's sake! Roman collar and all!
GEORGE	He wanted the cuffs done and the trousers taken up a bit.

GEORGE PULLS ACROSS A CURTAIN TO REVEAL -

And there it is...

SENAN	Ah, no. No...
GEORGE	And his gaberdine. 'Wanted that hemmed and the lining stitched. I sent the lot out to be dry-cleaned and when it came back I told him...
SENAN	(HOPELESS) No...
GEORGE	'Reminded him, more than once...
SENAN	So he must... has to be gone in, in civvies...
GEORGE	'Looks like it... 'Easy enough to mend a habit, replace the bits that's frayed... But if this is what I think it is, there'll be no mending it - in this world, anyway...

SCENE 9   THE COMMUNITY ROOM.

HUGO SITS SMOKING... DECLAN APPROACHES WITH THE MORNING PAPERS...

DECLAN	Ah, Father Hugo. You weren't long over your breakfast.
HUGO	The talk in the Refectory, Declan - I gave it a miss.

HE DROPS THE NEWSPAPERS ON AN OCCASIONAL TABLE.

DECLAN	More doom and gloom...
HUGO:	Ah, good man yourself.
DECLAN	Oh, dear. Ash trays... glasses, empties -

HUGO	Ah, we fought the good fight last night, Declan. 'Solved all the problems of the Universe…
DECLAN	Will I open a window atself?
HUGO	And let out the bit o' heat? No thanks, Brother.
DECLAN	Well… Matthew will be along after serving the nine, he'll clear up...
HUGO	(LEAFING THROUGH NEWSPAPER.) No doubt, the Irish Times has come on a lot since Vatican Two…
DECLAN	Now... I'm away. Brother John rang the Sacristy a few minutes ago to say he had Father Emmanuel up and dressed - you know yourself what that means...
HUGO	He'll insist on saying Mass.
DECLAN	I'd say they're heading for the lift this minute... Oh, I wouldn't mind if he'd settle for the Oratory. But no. 'Has to be a side altar in the Sanctuary.
HUGO	He's hanging in there, Declan. 'See us all down yet.
DECLAN	One of these days he'll keel over and give the people an awful fright.
HUGO	Full circle, Dec. He's on his way back to the cradle.
DECLAN	Oh, Brother John's the one that knows all about it... 'A full-time job looking after him - day and night...

SCENE TEN   **PRIOR'S OFFICE**

A WIRELESS/TRANSISTOR. MUGGY RECEPTION...

The Taoiseach, Mr. Lynch and the British Prime Minister-

MARK SWITCHES OFF RADIO AS FINTAN ENTERS -

MARK	Ah, Fintan... Spot on.
FINTAN	I wish I could say the same about my Canon Law.
MARK	A bit rusty, huh?.. Sit down, sit down.
FINTAN	Thank you.
MARK	So anyway... What did you dig up?
FINTAN	Eh-hh, I tried a few commentaries... Bouscaren and Ellis are about the -
MARK	Right, right.
FINTAN	They make a distinction -
MARK	Indeed.
FINTAN	- between a religious who deserts without the intention of returning and one who deserts -
MARK	With the intention of returning.
FINTAN	Have you been boning up, too, Father?
MARK	To be honest with you, Fintan, I've spent the last hour on the 'phone - one hospital after another.
FINTAN	Hospitals?
MARK	The Mater, Vincent's, Jervis Street, the Richmond... Well, you never know. A car crash. Maybe took ill, passed out somewhere...
FINTAN	You're joking?
MARK	I've done it, Father. And I'll keep trying, leave no stone

	unturned -
FINTAN	God love you.
FINTAN	'Loves me, you, us... Xavier. Yes, Xavier. Especially - for all I know - Xavier. And the same God tells us - tells me - to leave the ninty nine that are safe and go in search of the one that is... Anyway?
FINTAN	Well… what it boils down to is this: the intention of a religious who leaves his community, deserts the cloister, without permission...
MARK	What he has in mind.
FINTAN	That's it. If he skips intending to return he's a fugitive.
MARK	Ah! And if he cuts loose with no intention of -
FINTAN	The term is apostate. Apostate from the religious life.
MARK	So Xavier is one or the other...
FINTAN	Or neither. We just don't know.
MARK	Anything else?
FINTAN	The time factor.
MARK	Ah-hh... Tell me.
FINTAN	A month, give or take. If we don't hear from him in the next four weeks - if he doesn't contact us to say he intends to come back - then a presumption of law is established.
MARK	Come again?
FINTAN	'Means he has to be regarded as an apostate.
MARK	And the penalty?
FINTAN	Excommunication.
MARK	Jesus!
FINTAN	Reserved to the Major Superior.
MARK	The Provincial.
FINTAN	The man himself.

MARK	Now look, to get it right, exactly right -
FINTAN	Go ahead -
MARK	No word for a calander month… we presume he left without intending to return, declare him an apostate?
FINTAN	Correct... Or if he does something that would indicate that he doesn't intend to come back -
MARK	Like what?
FINTAN	Oh-hh... Taking up a job - secular employment, they call it - or getting engaged or, or -
MARK	Married?
FINTAN	Yes. It's called placing an act which can admit of no other interpretation.
MARK	So the ball's in his court, huh?
FINTAN	All we can do now is wait and see.
MARK	And pray...

SCENE 11   A CORRIDOR

EMMANUEL AND JOHN.

JOHN   Here we are, Father. Just mind your step.

MANUEL   Yes, yes, yes...

JOHN   I'll just hold on to you -

EMMANUEL   I'm not an invalid, you know.

JOHN   Sure, I know that, Father. Still, we don't want you losing
              your balance, now do we?

MANUEL   'Per-perfectly capable of walking by myself.

JOHN   Indeed... Easy does it... Ah, but it's the grey day out. Grey
              and cold and raining hard...

MANUEL   Pu-huh. 'Ever any other way in this miserable town?..
              Now Prague. Ah, Prague. There was a city...

JOHN   So you were saying.

MANUEL   No, no, not new Prague. The old city. Old Prague... I
              studied there, you know...

JOHN   Do you tell me?

MANUEL   'Best years of my life, really.

JOHN   Ah, ha...

MANUEL   Where, where are we?

JOHN   Ah, you know well, Father. We're on the ground floor of
              the Cloister... When we turn the corner we'll be at the door
              to the Sanctuary…

MANUEL   San-sanctuary...

JOHN   Sure we walk this corridor every morning…

MANUEL   Ah, yes... I remember now... Prague. Old Prague...

30

PRIOR'S OFFICE (CONT'D)

MARK   A month, huh. A month from today... Is he mad or what? 'Gone off his rocker altogether?.. And yet, for all we know, he could be out there somewhere, in dire straits...

FINTAN   I doubt that somehow... doubt it very much.

KNOCK ON OFFICE DOOR. MARK CALLS:

MARK   Come in...

HUGO ENTERS

HUGO   Oh? Sorry, I -

MARK   Come ahead, Hugo. He's not hearing my confession.

FINTAN   'Morning, Hugo.

HUGO   'Fintan... No, it's just, I thought I'd remind you, Prior -

MARK   What?

HUGO   Justin. He rang from London to say -

MARK   Yes, of course! Justin!

HUGO   'Due in this afternoon.

MARK   'Had a few days for himself after the hike from Jo'burg.

FINTAN   He'll have to be met.

MARK   Well, of course, but...

HUGO   I'll go if you like?..

MARK   Would you?! Best book one of the cars, so.

HUGO   I eh, already have - as a precaution, like.

MARK   God, Hugo, you don't miss a trick!

FINTAN   And while you're out at the airport you can check the

	passenger lists - all flights to London in the past -
MARK	Ah ha! Now you're hurling!..
HUGO	'Thought o' that, too. But it's no dice. Aer Lingus won't give out passanger information.
FINTAN	Oh?
HUGO	Policy... But I reckon I have a way round it.
MARK	Tell us...
HUGO	'Great friend of mine in the Special Branch -
MARK	Ha! You'll be telling us next you won the Sweep!.. Were you on to him?
HUGO	'Wasn't there but I left a message. He'll get back to me, no bother.
MARK	Good man... You're very quiet there, Fintan?
FINTAN	Hmmm?.. Oh, I was just... Weren't they students together, Justin and Xavier?
HUGO	Students together?! Fintan, they were ordained in Rome the same morning. 'Great friends over the years. If ever there was a particular friendship - God forgive me for judging! - it was them two!
FINTAN	I don't envy you so, meeting him off the plane...

SCENE 13   XAVIER'S ROOM...

SENAN AND GEORGE.

SENAN	His typewriter? What did he have, a portable?
GEORGE	Aye. Good little yoke it was, too. An Italian job... 'Always kept it over here, the press by his window... Oh, no!..
SENAN	What?
GEORGE	Someone got here before us, Senan.
SENAN	Maybe he took it with him?..
GEORGE	'Could be...
SENAN	'Would come in handy enough.
GEORGE	He was always a dab hand with the pen. And if he decides to write about what it was like, the inside story -
SENAN	Oh, stop, George! -
GEORGE	He has eighteen years, student and priest, to go on.
SENAN	Holy God! That's all we need! A series of articles in one o' them English Sunday papers!..
GEORGE:	Wouldn't put it past him! And if he needs the money?..
SENAN:	Dirt! Oh, dirt!
GEORGE:	Aye, and filth!.. Filth!

SCENE 14　　　　**DUBLIN AIRPORT**

INSIDE... AS IT WAS IN THE 60'S.

FEMALE ANNOUNCER ON INTERCOM:

"Will Mrs. Deasy, a passanger on Aer Lingus Flight EI 112 to Manchester, please go to the nearest red telephone... Mrs. Deasy..."

JUSTIN APPEARS FROM "ARRIVALS," PUSHING A TROLLEY:
ON IT, SUITCASE, HAND LUGGAGE, ETC.
HE STOPS, LOOKS AROUND.
HUGO, APPROACHING, WAVES TO JUSTIN.
THEY MEET UP.
HUGO IN HABIT, JUSTIN IN CIVVIES...

HUGO	Justin!
JUSTIN	Hugo!? Thanks for coming.
HUGO	Nearly didn't make it - the traffic!
JUSTIN	Ah, it's good to see you!
HUGO	And great to see you looking so well!
JUSTIN	Oh, thank you. Home sweet home, eh? 'Like stepping into another world.
HUGO	How long were you - ?
JUSTIN	Five years. 'My second stint.
HUGO	'Long old journey from Jo'burg. You must be bunched.
JUSTIN	'Not too bad. The few days in Rome broke it for me.
HUGO	Eh - here, let me push that. The car's not far, I'll bring it round to the entrance, save you getting wet.

JUSTIN	Don't tell me it's raining! In Dublin? Never!
HUGO	'Fraid so…
JUSTIN	So where did you get the tan?
HUGO	Ah, golf - what else? Wind from the sea...
JUSTIN	You've taken it up?
HUGO	'While ago.
JUSTIN	It's allowed, now?
HUGO	As long as you're eh, discreet. The Prior turns a blind eye...
JUSTIN	About bloody time. Well, we must give it a lash. Maybe get Xavier out. Does he play at all?
HUGO	Eh-hh. He does yeah, now and again. But he eh, he's very erratic.
JUSTIN	I can imagine! Hitting everything except the ball! Gas bloody man!.. We were students together, y'know. 'Know him like the back of my hand…
HUGO	Eh-hh… Tell you what, Justin: I know a place on the way into town, 'do a nice line in coffee. Quiet. Are you game?
JUSTIN	I'm easy… 'The brethren can wait.
HUGO:	That's if you're buying?!..
JUSTIN	Ah, I mighta known there'd be a catch.
HUGO	Y'know what they say: once a mendicant…

SCENE 15   PRIOR'S OFFICE...

FINTAN   Are you sure you want me to do this, Prior?
MARK   Ah... I suppose. Yeah, do. Do in the name o' God.

FINTAN LIFTS THE RECEIVER, DIALS SEVERAL DIGITS...

             If I did, she'd smell a rat. 'Coming from you...

FINTAN   Hello?.. Missus Crilly?... Father Fintan, here. Fintan, that's
             right... Yes!.. Ah, now you have me!

             No, I'll tell you, I'm ringing from out of town, trying to
             contact Xavier - he's not there with you by any chance?..
             No... Oh, no, not to worry... I'll track him down when I get
             back to base... Hmmm?... Oh, not at all, no urgency in the
             wide world...

             Oh, he is, in great form altogether. .. Has he been to see
             you lately?.. No. No, well, he's kept going, I can tell you...
             I will to be sure. .. Oh, indeed... and he's very proud of
             you, too, Ma'am... Oh, I'm going to be cut off! God bless
             now, Missus Crilly... God bless...

FINTAN REPLACES THE RECEIVER. DRAINED...

             Ph-e-e-e—www!..

MARK	Hmmm... If the divil came to look for a liar, Fintan, I don't know where we'd hide you...
FINTAN	'Hated doing it, I don't mind telling you...
MARK	Ah, a venial sin at the most. 'Had to be done. And thank you, Father. At least we know now...
FINTAN	She hasn't seen her adoring son for months.
MARK	'Going senile, is she? Sure he went home after Christmas.
FINTAN	Oh, yeah?
MARK	Well, I'm the one that gave him leave... Ah, bloody Hell! So where was he? A whole week?!..
FINTAN	'Way ahead of you, Mark.
MARK	'Beginning to think he was way ahead of us all...

SCENE 16   **LOUNGE BAR**

HUGO AND JUSTIN SEATED IN A QUIET CORNER... COFFEE...

JUSTIN	So... That's the score...
HUGO	'Half time, anyway...
JUSTIN	Jesus... Jesus Christ...
HUGO	Amen.
JUSTIN	Oh-hh... Maybe it's kicking the arse off you I should be this minute.

HUGO	Wh-what?
JUSTIN	All that small talk, letting me rabbit on!
HUGO	Ah, God, Justin, I was only for the best! 'Didn't know what way to, to go about -
JUSTIN	Okay. It's okay... I, I understand. 'Not easy for you to... It's just - I don't, I can't believe... Oh-hh-hh. . . Jesus. Jesus wept...
HUGO	I, I know how you feel.
JUSTIN	Do you? 'Ever lose a brother - sudden death?
HUGO	No, but I -
JUSTIN	He was brother to me, I to him. Almost blood you might say, the bond between us. Maybe stronger, for all I know...
HUGO	Yeah, I was just saying to the -
JUSTIN	I loved him, Hugo. . . What am I saying? I love him still. 'Suppose I always will... no matter what... God, I could do with a drink.
HUGO	'Makes two of us...

SCENE 17   **THE REFECTORY**

BROTHERS JOHN, SENAN, GEORGE SEATED AT TABLE.

JOHN	What?!... You're joking. Say you're joking.
SENAN	It'd be a very sick joke...
JOHN	But I mean, are you sure?
GEORGE	Just about. Oh, there's an outside chance that... but I wouldn't bet on it. All the signs, like, are pointing the same way...
JOHN	Jesus, Mary and Joseph!..
SENAN	You might as well make it a prayer, John, while you're at it -
JOHN	Guide and protect him, keep him on the straight and narrow.
SENAN	'Tis far from the straight and narrow he is, be the looks of it.
JOHN	I don't... I just can't...
GEORGE	Young fool. Young bloody fool.
SENAN	It's a wonder you didn't get wind of it before now. Ah, more time in the kitchen, John, and less time with Emmanuel…
GEORGE	Where is he now, anyway?
JOHN	Hmmm?.. Oh, I - I left him reading in the Library.
SENAN	'Safe enough. As long as he doesn't stand up...
JOHN	Oh, dear... Dear, dear, dear... Oh, I knew he was a bit on the wild side. And you'd need to be blind not to see he was cutting a few corners. But to go and?..
SENAN	Ah, the divil got into him.

GEORGE	Now you're talking, Senan. Got at him - through a woman.
SENAN	A she-devil. Be god, huh?..
JOHN	Now we don't know that for sure. You're jumping the gun.
SENAN	You only have to go up to his room, take a look for yourself.
GEORGE	Dumped what he didn't want, packed what he did.
SENAN	Left his habit on the back of the door.
GEORGE	Planned. The whole thing thought out. Well in advance.
SENAN	And when the rest of us were asleep he, he made his move.
GEORGE	'Slipped out the side-door. Her waiting for him in a car... taxi, mebbe...
SENAN	And then what, huh? What do you reckon?
GEORGE	Oh. . . Overnight in some house... Maybe a hotel or a B and B...
SENAN	'Could be, huh. Him in civvies...
GEORGE	And when he was supposed to be saying Mass on the High altar he was boarding an Aer Lingus for London.
SENAN	Sick! Ah, sick! A sick, sorry mess!
JOHN	Now wait a minute! How much of this is, is?.. I mean, do we know for a fact how or when or who with? Or are ye making it up as ye go along?

SCENE 18   THE LOUNGE.

HUGO AND JUSTIN DRINKING…

JUSTIN   Oh, we went different ways and I didn't see all that much
            of him after Rome. He was sent down the country and I
            volunteered for South Afica. And I was never a great man
            for writing letters. The few times he wrote and I wrote
            back there was never a hint of anything…

HUGO   'Kept it to himself.

JUSTIN   'Takes a bit out of you, I suppose, to open up to another
            priest outside of Confession. What am I saying? 'Know
            bloody well it does...

HUGO   We all have our pride. And when that's hurt...

JUSTIN   'Enough said.

HUGO   Anyway, who's to say for sure he wanted help? He knew
            only too well the advice he'd get.

JUSTIN   Physician, heal thyself, huh? "Get the girl out of the
            picture. You won't be able to think straight as long as
            she's in the frame."

HUGO   A good retreat somewhere. A Monastery, mebbe.

JUSTIN   Or a change, altogether...

HUGO   'Fresh start, eh. Ah, I'd say he was afraid of a transfer - no
            more than myself.

JUSTIN   'Same where I am. We all put down roots, make friends,
            get set in our ways. It's only human...

HUGO   God, I'd say it's just about impossible to go it alone. If you
            didn't have a friend or two out there you'd go bananas...

SCENE 19   PRIOR'S OFFICE

MARK AT HIS DESK. HE LOOKS UP AS FINTAN ENTERS...

MARK	Ah, Fintan. Any sign of it slackening?
FINTAN	Not much. But you never know when you're on duty...
MARK	Ah, well... Only another few hours. I'd swap with you any day.
FINTAN	How do y'mean?
MARK	I'm the whole afternoon doing the books. A right pain in the...
FINTAN	It's an accountant you should have been.
MARK	Them fellas make money, not shell it out...
FINTAN	Any word?
MARK	Not a whisper.
FINTAN	I may be wrong but I think some of our regulars are beginning to wonder...
MARK	Oh?..
FINTAN	Just a feeling I have. Some of the ould wans stopping me to ask how he is, is he all right?..
MARK	Oh oh...
FINTAN	Looking me in the eye. They've noticed he hasn't said Mass on the High Altar - or been out to hear confessions.
MARK	God, is there anything they don't notice? 'Live in your ear if you let them...
FINTAN	Any sign of Justin yet?
MARK	'Should have been here before now. Unless the flight was delayed - or he was waylaid.

FINTAN   What?

MARK   Well, Hugo was more than a bit keen to meet him...

BUZZAR SOUNDS, OFF: TWO SHORTS AND A LONG...

FINTAN   Ah, here we go again! If it's another Maternity Blessing
            I'll scream!

MARK   It's a long old formula, right enough.

FINTAN   A pregnancy couldn't be much longer...

SCENE 20   THE LOUNGE... G AND T'S...

JUSTIN   He was giving the hard stuff a lash, huh?

HUGO   Maybe more than was good for him. But who am I to talk?
            I'm no angel...

JUSTIN   So... he met her and they hit it off. One thing led to
            another...

HUGO   That's the story.

JUSTIN   What's she like? 'Know anything about her?

HUGO   'Met her once or twice. Good looking, yeah. Attractive.

JUSTIN   But will she be good for him? Y'know, like - will she look
            after him?

HUGO	That I couldn't say. More than a bit on the wild side. And fond of the jar, you could see that. A glass in one hand, a fag in the other.
JUSTIN	I'm beginning to get the picture... Religion?
HUGO	Not much. A strong, anti-clerical strain in her family.
JUSTIN	Hmmm... So if Xavier came out?
HUGO	Oh, I'd say they gave three cheers...
JUSTIN	He was drinking with her, huh? Hotels, late nights - all that?
HUGO	And out in her house. As long as she had the money.
JUSTIN	He would have made a contribution. Presents, personal gifts. Maybe even dipped into the Mass money...
HUGO	Maybe... I, I have to be careful here.
JUSTIN	What?
HUGO	He, he came into my room a few times... for absolution.
JUSTIN	Oh... Right.
HUGO	Y'know, Justin, there's a breed of female that are drawn to priests, religious. I dunno if you -
JUSTIN	I do. Be God, don't I! They crop up everywhere. And damned if they'd be bothered with an ordinary bloke. 'Has to be someone - inaccessible.
HUGO	Forbidden fruit.
JUSTIN	Out to take you over, organise you.
HUGO	Possessive.
JUSTIN	Oh, if you let down your guard at all you're finished... So you reckon she's out of that stable?
HUGO	Bull's eye.
JUSTIN	Hmmm... Will you go another?
HUGO	Eh-hh… The Prior's expecting you.

44

JUSTIN	Fair enough.
HUGO	And he'll surely give Recreation tonight in your honour.
JUSTIN	I'll be meeting them all, then. And they all know?
HUGO	I'd say they can talk about nothing else... Come on, I'll show you Nelson's Pillar while there's still light - what's left of it...

SCENE 21   THE REFECTORY. SIDE TABLE.

SENAN	'Like wild fire once it gets out. No stopping it.
JOHN	And his mother still alive, God help us.
GEORGE	It'll kill her when she finds out. Aye, surely.
SENAN	Small town. She won't be able to lift her head.
JOHN	She'll go under the bed clothes.
GEORGE	He might as well have coffined her.
JOHN	Did he stop to think, I wonder, about the shame and the -
GEORGE	That's just it. There was himself and herself and that was their world.
SENAN	They say love is blind.
GEORGE	What's love got to do with it? Lust, that's what it is - lust!
JOHN	Ah, God, Brother George, you're very hard on him -
GEORGE	I call a spade a spade. And I can tell you, Brother John, if

	it's what I think it is - if a member of this Community has gone off with his lady friend - then it stinks!
SENAN	Oh, be gor, huh! You're getting into your stride now all right!
GEORGE	Stinks of selfishness and immaturity and, and irresponsibility!
SENAN	Ho, ho! There's a quare mouthful for you!
GEORGE	And I'll remind you, Brother Senan - not that you should need reminding - that this is far from a laughing matter.
SENAN	Sorry. Sorry, Brother, I -
GEORGE	We're into scandal here, scandal with a capital S...

NOISE OFF...

JOHN	What was that?
GEORGE	What?
JOHN	I thought I heard a -

DECLAN HURRIES IN -

DECLAN	Quick! Come quick! -
SENAN	What is it? -
DECLAN	Emmanuel! -
JOHN	Move, move! -
DECLAN	On the floor -
GEORGE	Hurry!
DECLAN	'Can't lift him on my own!

THEY HURRY OFF, AD-LIBBING...

SCENE 22   PRIOR'S OFFICE.

MARK... HUGO APPROACHES.

MARK	Ah, Hugo... Justin get in all right?
HUGO	Safe and sound.
MARK	So where is he now?
HUGO	On the ground floor. Soon as we got in the door -
MARK	He was ambushed.
HUGO	Getting a great welcome, I can tell you.
MARK	And looking the picture of health, no doubt.
HUGO	Blooming.
MARK	So... how did he take it?
HUGO	Got one Helluva shock. We-we'd still be nursing G and T's if I hadn't put the skids under him.
MARK	Understandable... (MOVING) 'Better go down and -
HUGO	Eh-hh... When I was coming back round from the garage, Prior, I thought I saw Doctor Riordan driving away?..
MARK	Be Gor, Hugo, you don't miss much...
HUGO	Emmanuel?
MARK	Yeah, he fell again. In the Library. 'Luck o'God, Declan was passing. John and Senan gave him a hand and George rang me...
HUGO	So where is he now?
MARK	Back in his room. We managed to get him into bed. Just about. You'd never think to look at him, he was so heavy...
HUGO:	And the doctor?
MARK	'Says it's the blood pressure - and the diabetis isn't

	helping. But the heart is still strong. 'Could go any minute… or then again...
HUGO	'Hard to know what to say.
MARK:	Or do... I've told the Brothers he's not to say Mass. For another while, anyhow... 'See how it goes.
HUGO	I know John is Infirmarian but that's a far cry from... I mean, he can change a bandage, dish out a few aspirin, but he has no real training -
MARK	'Not fair on him.
HUGO	Or on Emmanuel.
MARK	'Not fair on any of us... Well, something will have to be done and per usual it'll be up to me to, to…
HUGO	God love you, Mark.
MARK	And if he does, he has a funny bloody way of showing it...

SCENE 23   THE KITCHEN

SENAN BUSY – POTS, PANS, ETC. SINGING A SNATCH OR TWO
FROM "MARY ANNE..." A DISGRUNTLED GILES BLUSTERS IN...

GILES:	Well bad luck to them, anyway!
SENAN	Wh-what? Who?
GILES	Them that run the Rosslare to Dublin, that's who! No heating and no diner - I couldn't even get a cup of tea!.. And not even the glimmer of an apology!.. Is that kettle boiled, Senan?
SENAN	Well, it is, Father, it is. Sure I always keep it on standby -
GILES	'Tis a hot whiskey I should be having - before I sink into double pneumonia altogether...
SENAN	Ah, God love you, anyhow -
GILES	Anyway... when all fruit fails, welcome hobs...
SENAN	Here, y'are now, Father.

SENAN OFFERS A CUP OF TEA... SUGAR, MILK.

GILES	Ah, good man, good man yourself... Oh, I should have known...
SENAN	Father?
GILES	That's the last time I'll go down in winter to the brother's farm.
SENAN	Rough, was it?
GILES	Ah-hh! When I didn't get me death! Oh, they had a fire in the kitchen, sure enough, but the rest of the house was ice. Going to bed was a pure penance.

SENAN	Be gor, that's grim, all right.
GILES	They never heard of central heating in Taghmon...
SENAN	Eh, if I'm not greatly mistaken, Father Giles, you weren't due back till the weekend?
GILES	'Cut it short. Enough's enough. When you get to my age, Senan, you can only take so much...
SENAN	I know, yeah...
GILES	'Anyone in my room?
SENAN	No. No, it's waiting for you.
GILES	Good, good. What I'll do, then, I'll go up and lie down for an hour, get the chill out of me bones.
SENAN	Would you like me to make you a hot water bottle, Father?
GILES	Would you? Would you, Brother?
SENAN	No sooner said than done.
GILES	Ah, no doubt, there's a great streak in you, Senan.
SENAN	Be gor, then, you're the first that ever said that to me! So... will you be back on your feet in time for Recreation?
GILES	What?
SENAN	For Father Justin.
GILES	Oh, he's with us, is he?
SENAN	Just flew in. Hale and hearty.
GILES	Hmmm... 'Best o' both worlds. Where is he now?
SENAN	'Don't rightly know. 'Went upstairs with the Prior -
GILES	Huh... 'In his office, I suppose. 'Conclave...
SENAN	Here y'are now, Father Giles. Piping hot...

SENAN CROSSES TO GILES, HOT WATER BOTTLE IN HAND...

GILES	Ah. me life on you, Senan.

SENAN	I'll just wrap it in a towel...
GILES	So... what else is new?
SENAN	Eh-hh-hh... Father Xavier...
GILES	Huh... What is he up to this time?
SENAN	Well, that's just it. We don't rightly know.
GILES	What?
SENAN	We, we think he's gone.
GILES	How do y'mean?
SENAN	Gone, Father Giles. Gone altogether...

SCENE 24   A CORRIDOR...

MARK. JUSTIN CARRYING/WHEELING A SUIT CASE.

MARK	This way, Father Justin... Sure the place hasn't changed much since you were here last...
JUSTIN	Indeed, no.
MARK	God knows, it could do with a lick of paint. But that's the least of my worries...
JUSTIN	I'm sure...
MARK	Along here now... We put you in Edward's room - for now, anyway. He's away giving a Retreat to a flock of nuns and then he's taking a few days off...

JUSTIN	He'll need it...
MARK	Back of the house so the traffic won't keep you awake at night... Xavier's room just across the corridor.
JUSTIN	Really? Is it locked?
MARK	No. No, it's not. 'Want to take a look?
JUSTIN	Please, yes... if I may...
MARK	Not that there's much to see -

THEY ENTER XAVIER'S ROOM

	Step in... He left it tidy enough - for a man in a hurry... Ah, God, would you believe that?
JUSTIN	Hmmm?
MARK	His radio. A transistor. 'Gone...
JUSTIN	Maybe he took it with him?
MARK	No. No, it was here this morning when I was... Wouldn't you think they'd have the?..
JUSTIN	Someone didn't lose much time.
MARK	Ah, I won't say it -

BUZZAR: TWO LONGS AND A SHORT...

	Oh, that's me... Make yourself at home, Justin, and if there's anything I can do for you, don't hesitate...
JUSTIN	Ah, thank you, Prior.
MARK	We'll have a deoram in the Community Room after supper.

JUSTIN	Great... 'See you, then.
MARK	(GOING) Welcome, Justin...

JUSTIN TURNS BACK, BEGINS TO TAKE STOCK.
HE MOVES AROUND, PAUSING HERE AND THERE TO CHECK,
INSPECT, OPEN AND CLOSE... HE SITS AT THE DESK, OPENS
ONE DRAWER, THEN ANOTHER... HE LIFTS A BUNDLE/SHEAF
OF DOCUMENTS FROM A DRAWER, PLACES IT ON THE DESK,
BEGINS TO SIFT THROUGH IT...

SCENE 25   THE RECTOR'S OFFICE

... PHONE ON DESK RINGING... MARK ENTERS, HURRIES
ACROSS TO ANSWER, LIFTS RECEIVER...

MARK   Yes, Cecil, what?.. Hmmm... Well, if he won't give his
name..? Eh-hh-hh... All right, then... I'll take it on line
two... (PAUSE)
Hello?.. 'Speaking... Finnegan... Well, what can I do for
you, Mister Finnegan?.. Father Xavier... He what?.. Well...
it, it's not usual... Can I ask how much you?.. I see... Did
he mention this, eh, deserving cause?.. No. No, that's all

right... And your number is... Six, eight... ah, ha... 'have that... office hours... I'll get back to you if... Oh, I do. I appreciate your concern... And thank you for ringing...

MARK CRADLES THE RECEIVER, STANDS A LONG MOMENT...

God... Deserving cause... Oh, dear God in Heaven...

SCENE 26 **GILES'S ROOM**

GILES ENTERS, SETS DOWN HIS SUITCASE/HOLD-ALL...
WHEEZING, MUTTERING TO HIMSELF...

HE CROSSES TO HIS BED... INSERTS THE HOTWATER BOTTLE
BETWEEN THE SHEETS... SITS...

GILES   Huh... Huh!.. Doesn't surprise me... doesn't surprise me...
        A pup! 'Proper pup! 'Would never do what he was told,
        never! Oh, a brat if ever there was one... 'Carried it too far,
        the joking and the jeering!..

Made fun of me in front of the Community... at Recreation
one night... 'Could never forget the hurt! Unforgivable the
way he went on - sent me up rotten!

Ah, I suppose I managed a smile at the time - the others
thought it was hilarious - but underneath I was in a terrible
tantrum… raging...

HE KICKS OFF HIS SHOES… PULLS THE COWL OF HIS HABIT UP
OVER HIS HEAD AND OFF… SETS IT ASIDE.

Please God now I'll sleep... and with a bit of luck... I'll
wake in time for Recreation...

SCENE 27   PRIOR'S OFFICE

MARK ON THE PHONE…

MARK   Hello?.. Father Joe?.. Joe, this is Mark... Ah, sill above
            ground... And yourself?.. That's the spirit…
            Look, eh, one of the men here, one of the youngest...
            Right, yes... Bingo… He, he's made a, an exit... All the
            signs are, for good… And may be with a friend - if you
            know what I mean...

And just now I had a call from a business man here in town. He was conned by you know who… parted with fifty notes… 'Told it was for a good cause... I may be wrong but that could mean two singles to Heathrow...

That's right, funds could run out quicker than... Well, you're the obvious... He may not, of course, but if he does?.. Ah, that's great...

Any help you give him, we'll make it up to you this end…'Not an easy job, this, I'll tell you... What, sorry?.. Oh, for sure… Bye for now… Bye, Joe…

HE SETS DOWN THE RECEIVER…

I wouldn't like to see him out on the street… no matter what…

SCENE 28   THE KITCHEN...

SENAN BUSY... JOHN APPROACHES...

JOHN	Oh, I could kick myself this minute...
SENAN	What?
JOHN	Ah-hh... Father Emmanuel.
SENAN	Now, come on, Brother John! Have a bit o' sense, will you? You're no more to blame -
JOHN	It's on my mind -
SENAN	'Left him for a few minutes, that's all. Sure, who could blame you for taking a break?..
GEORGE	(APPROACHING) Blame?.. Blame!.. Who's getting it in the neck this time?
SENAN	You can't be with him morning, noon and night - can he, George?
GEORGE	Emmanuel?.. 'Deed and he can't. 'John taking it out on himself?
SENAN	You only have to look at his face...
JOHN	It's just... I should have known better than to leave him on his own in the Library.
GEORGE	What are you supposed to have - a crystal ball?
SENAN	'You sick with the worry and him above in the bed, not a bother on him. Huh!
GEORGE	You've nothing to blame yourself for, Brother John, nothing - not a thing in the world!
SENAN	It's too much you're doing for him if the truth was told.
GEORGE	Give it here to me, John. I'm finished in the Tailory so I've a bit o' slack before supper.

GEORGE TAKES THE TRAY FROM JOHN...

	You just take it handy for a while like a good man.
SENAN	Ah, that's the spirit, Brother!
JOHN	Are you, are you sure?..
GEORGE	Will you go way before I change my mind!
JOHN	Well, then, I... I'll just finish my Office on the top corridor.
GEORGE	You can go up to the Television Room and gawk at Blue Peter for all I mind...

SCENE 29   A CORRIDOR.

JOHN MOVING SLOWLY, FINGERING BEADS.
AIDAN APPROACHES...

JOHN	Ah, Father Aidan. 'Back from the teaching...
AIDAN	Yes... It, it was a long day.
JOHN	And the day that's in it. You must be perished.
AIDAN :	I'm all in to tell the truth.
JOHN	It's taking it out of you, I can see that.
AIDAN	My privilege - that's how I look at it.
JOHN	Father?..
AIDAN	Wonderful Apostolate. Teaching Christian

58

	Doctrine to Dublin's underprivileged poor...
JOHN	Ah, but do they listen?
AIDAN	Some. Some do. I - I feel I'm getting through…
JOHN	And the rest?..
AIDAN	Well... all we can do is try...
JOHN	More than Father Xavier did be all accounts - God love him, anyhow.
AIDAN	Sorry?..
JOHN	Oh?.. You didn't hear?
AIDAN	Hear what?
JOHN	He, he's gone. Gone for good. And not a word to anyone.
AIDAN	(AGITATED) I... I...
JOHN	Oh, sorry. God, sorry, Father Aidan. Maybe I shouldn't have -
AIDAN	(BESIDE HIMSELF) Oh-hh-hh... Oh-hh-hh...
JOHN	Father?.. God, Father -
AIDAN	Tell me he's dead! Say he's dead!
JOHN	Well, well he is in a way - to us, anyhow...
AIDAN	Gone?.. Left?!..
JOHN	Yes... Well, we reckon -
AIDAN	And you're not - ? This, this isn't a sick, sick joke?!..
JOHN	No. No, Father -
AIDAN	Then would to God - oh, would to God! - you were telling me he was cold and laid out and awaiting Requiem!
JOHN	Ah, Father, you mustn't -
AIDAN	This, this - if what you tell me be true and not mere conjecture - then it's worse, far worse, than any death -
JOHN	I'm sorry, Father Aidan, I didn't know, couldn't see how, how upset you -

AIDAN	Upset? Upset?!..
JOHN	Please, Father, calm yourself -
AIDAN	I'm out there, day after school day, teaching, trying to -
JOHN	Hush, Father, hush -
AIDAN	Coming back here to, to -
JOHN	Ah, Lord, Father, I didn't mean to -
AIDAN	To what? A constant struggle to, to -
JOHN	Father Aidan, I -
AIDAN	Back to the mediocre, the mundane - there, I've said it!
JOHN	Father, you'll raise the corridor -
AIDAN	Those boys, some of them, are tomorrow's priests. I, I explain to them about celibacy...
JOHN	To be sure you do -
AIDAN	And then he goes and -
JOHN	I, I mebbe should tell you, Father Giles is having a bit of a siesta.
AIDAN	(PAUSE... DRIPPING SARCASM) Father Giles is having a siesta... a bit of a siesta...
JOHN	So - so Brother Senan was saying -
AIDAN	Well, we mustn't disturb him, must we? Otherwise he might be discommoded... maybe become disgruntled...
JOHN	Ah, sure, you know yourself his form.
AIDAN	Indeed... But do we know Xavier's form?
JOHN	Father?..
AIDAN	Is there..? Is there a, a female?..
JOHN	They say so. Yes. Yes, there -
AIDAN	(BESIDE HIMSELF... TURNING AWAY...) Ohh-hh-hh!.. Ohhh-hh-hhh!.
JOHN	(CALLING) Father?.. Father Aidan?!

SCENE 30   AIDAN'S ROOM

HE ENTERS, AGITATED…

DROPS HIS BRIEFCASE…

SEARCHES IN A DRAWER OF HIS DESK…

FINDS A PACKET OF CIGARETTES… MATCHES…

LIGHTS A CIGARETTE… INHALES…

AIDAN   So he is?.. So he is..?!

HE SLUMPS INTO A CHAIR…

             What am I going to say?!..
             What am I going to say to my students -
             when they get wind of it... as they surely will?..

             How do I answer when they ask -
             why him… and not me?..

SCENE 31   EMMANUEL'S ROOM

GEORGE ENTERS, HOLDING TRAY…

GEORGE   Hello?.. Father?.. Father Emmanuel?.. Are you there?..

MANUEL   Wh - ?.. What?!..

GEORGE   Easy now, Father, take it easy. No need to -

MANUEL   Who?.. Are, are you the Provincial?

GEORGE   Occhh, come on, Father! You can't be that bad! Sit up now
            like a good man and have a sup of this beef broth. It'll curl
            the hairs on your chest. Aye, surely…

MANUEL   What?.. What!?...

GEORGE   How are you feeling, anyway? Are you all right?

MANUEL   What! Of, of course I'm all right, you, you silly moo!

GEORGE   God, I've been called a quare few things in my time but
            never till now a silly moo... But you have a point, Father,
            sure you're as right as rain... 'Only have to look at you…
            Come on, now, have a spoonful of this. Do you good…

GEORGE SPOONING… EMMANUEL SLURPING, SWALLOWING…

            That's the man… that's the good -

MANUEL   Fa - Father Provincial?..

GEORGE   No, no, a leanna. I'm just a brother. That's it, that's it.
            You're doing nicely.

MANUEL   'Must… must see the Provincial…

GEORGE   Ah, well, now.. . 'Easier said than done, Father... One
            more spoonful and the job's oxo -

MANUEL   Tell him, it - it's urgent -

GEORGE	But sure he's not even in the house, Father. 'Away on Visitation. 'Far end of the country... And even if he was -
MANUEL	I - I was attacked, you see -
GEORGE	What?!
MANUEL	There were three, four of them -
GEORGE	Holy God!
MANUEL	'Knocked me to the ground, set, set upon me -
GEORGE	Never!
MANUEL	'Got into the, the cloister -
GEORGE	There's a wonder!
MANUEL	'Co-could be still here -
GEORGE	God between us and all harm!
MANUEL	He, he'll know what to do.
GEORGE	Who - the Provincial?
MANUEL	Who else, you dolt!
GEORGE	Yes. Aye, well... You leave it to me, Father. I'll have a scout around. 'Stand guard outside your door... They won't get past me, that's for sure... All night if I have to...
MANUEL	Poison...
GEORGE	What?
MANUEL	He, he was poisoned. O'Neill. The O'Neill.
GEORGE	Oh.
MANUEL	On the Ja-Janiculum. Looking down on, on Rome.
GEORGE	Poison.
MANUEL	A British agent put it in his, his wine...
GEORGE	I see.
MANUEL	That's how he, he went... Looking down at, at Rome...
GEORGE	Hmmm... Be gor, huh? What a way to go...

SCENE 32   XAVIER'S ROOM

JUSTIN SEATED AT DESK, READING A FILE, MSS.
DECLAN ENTERS. JUSTIN MOVES TO GREET HIM.

JUSTIN	Declan! Dear Brother Declan!
DECLAN	Ah, Father Justin! -
JUSTIN	Great to see you, my old friend! How have you been keeping?
DECLAN	Ah well, Father, well enough. I, I'm not getting any younger.
JUSTIN	You could have fooled me!

THEY MOVE INTO ROOM, SEAT THEMSELVES...

DECLAN	God, the colour! You didn't get that in any cloister.
JUSTIN	No, out and about. Always on the go. I have a big parish, Declan - and a thriving one, thanks be to God...
DECLAN	Ah, you did the right thing, Father, volunteering for Africa.
JUSTIN	I won't argue with that...
DECLAN	To be honest, I was on the corridor saying my office when I noticed the light under the door...
FINTAN	You were thinking - hoping - it might be Xavier?
DECLAN	And I'd be able to say my prayers were answered...
JUSTIN	I'm afraid he's gone from us, Declan.
DECLAN	Oh, dear. Dear, dear, dear. And won't be back?
JUSTIN	Maybe... When he comes to his senses... But I can't see him ever back - here...

DECLAN	God guide him wherever he is.
JUSTIN	You were very fond of him, Brother?
DECLAN	Ah, sure, how could you not be?! He always had the kind word, the smile, touch...
JUSTIN	Touch?
DECLAN	Ah... Now and again, he'd put a hand on my shoulder or give me a hug. And when I knelt for a blessing after serving his Mass, his hands would press, really press, on my head. Then he'd help me to my feet... Like, do y'know what I'm trying to say, Father?..
JUSTIN	Oh, indeed I do.
DECLAN	Touch seemed to mean a lot to him, though I don't think he was aware of it himself. As if he was always in search of, of affection...
JUSTIN	That'd be him all right...
DECLAN	The children from the tenaments. He'd never pass but he'd have a few sweets for them - and a pat on the head...
JUSTIN	So... who's to put a friendly hand on your shoulder now, Declan?
DECLAN	Ah, well... They're not all as warm as Father Xavier... Some of them, God help us, just can't show it - though underneath, sure, they're full of love... But no matter. One of these days the Good Lord will stretch out his hand and touch me, bring me home...
JUSTIN	Ah-hh... May he leave you with us for another good while.
DECLAN	Oh, I'll be glad to go, Father Justin. 'Glad I lived my life when I did... The Order is changing, the Church is changing. Change and more change. I can see it coming. Now I can... Well, I'm too old to change, Father. Too set

	in my ways. . . I just hope it'll work out, be for the better...
JUSTIN	It will, Brother, it will…
DECLAN	Oh, I'll tell you... between the two of us, 'not the first time I came in that door. Many's the time I knelt to him where you're sitting now...
JUSTIN	Ah ha...
DECLAN	Sure, you could tell him anything. Not that I had much to confess, God knows. Aye, and I wasn't the only one. A lot of the Brothers went to him - well, up until the word got round that he was, was going out a lot, like, doing things he mebbe shouldn't...
JUSTIN	Whatever his own sins, Declan, he was a good confessor.
DECLAN	He was - gentle... Once, when I was confessing to him, he put his hands on mine, whispered in my ear - "Tis me should be kneeling to you, Brother…"
JUSTIN	You could never forget... a gesture like that...
DECLAN	Sure, people came from miles around to go to him, did you know?
JUSTIN	I can well believe it.
DECLAN	'Rang up, some of them, to find out what Mass he was on of a Sunday - so they could get his sermon...
JUSTIN	I was just having a look for myself when you knocked. 'Put a lot of work into his preaching...
DECLAN	'Used to walk the corridor, there, up and down, getting it off by heart - when he had a Mission or a Retreat coming up... Ah, what happened him at all?
JUSTIN	He was his own worst enemy, 'about the height of it…

BELL/GONG SOUNDS IN DISTANCE

DECLAN   Oh... The bell for supper... I'll leave you and love you,
                    Father.

JUSTIN   God go with you, Brother Declan.

DECLAN   And with you, Father... and with you...

DECLAN LEAVES...

JUSTIN   Hmmm... Gentle, huh... There's gentle for you...
                    Gentleman... Holy man...
                    A few more like him and it would be a different Church...

SCENE 33

THE CHOIR. MEMBERS OF THE COMMUNITY KNEELING IN
SILENT PRAYER, MEDITATION.
SUDDEN SHARP ACOUSTIC: KNUCKLES ON WOOD. AT THIS
SIGNAL, A FRIAR (CANTOR) STANDS AND INTONES THE FIRST
LINE OF THE MISERERE:

Miserere mei, Deus...

THE OTHERS STAND, JOIN IN THE RECITATION OF THE PSALM:

secundum magnum misericordiam tuam... etc.

EVEN AS THEY BEGIN TO RECITE THEY STEP DOWN,
TWO BY TWO, FROM THE CHOIR STALLS... WALK FORWARD...
GENUFLECT TWO BY TWO... THEN TURN AND EXEUNT...
CALLING OUT THE *MISERERE* AS THEY DO SO...
A CHANT THAT GROWS FAINT... FAINTER...

SCENE 34   GILES ROOM

GILES STANDS AT THE MIRROR AND WASH BASIN, DRYING HIS
HANDS AND FACE WITH A TOWEL.
HE IS IN SHIRT, TROUSERS, BRACES... SLIPPERS...

GILES   Ah-hh... Oh-hh-hhh... That's it. Nothing like a freshen-up
                 after forty winks... New man, new man. 'Like starting the
                 day all over...

'

HE DISCARDS THE TOWEL, CROSSES TO THE DOOR TO WHERE HIS HABIT IS HANGING… LIFTS IT OFF THE HOOK, SLIPS IT FROM THE CLOTHES HANGER…

'Slip on the ould habit and I'll be ready for battle... 'Few stains down the front, lately, I notice. It'll be for the dry-cleaners before much longer...

HE FINISHES DRESSING: HABIT… THEN COWL…

They should be out of the Refectory soon. I'll slip down the back stairs to the kitchen, collar Senan before he has time to slip away. A bit of plamas and he'll do me a couple of chops, maybe a mixed grill... Ah-hh... That'll hit the spot...

'Bit of a stretch in the evenings, no doubt... The Lenten Missions will be starting soon... I always get one or two... Down the country... Simple people - not like the shower up here...

'Start them with the Four Last Things - Death, the Judgement, Heaven or Hell... 'Put the fear o' God into them... Still one of my favourite sermons. Great old stand-by…

And with any luck the Parish Priest will give me a warm welcome: roast beef, medium rare, the way I like it... 'glass of wine... Aye, and a good drop of the hard stuff... nightcap... eight hours' sleep guaranteed…

HE CROSSES TO HIS DESK, LIGHTS A CIGARETTE, INHALES.

Then, about the middle of the week, I'll give them my best sermon ever: the Mercy of God... Ah, yes... Mary Magdalene... the Prodigal Son... the Good Shepherd... 'Melt their hearts... 'Have them queuing outside my box...

SCENE 35   XAVIER'S ROOM

JUSTIN STILL SEATED AT DESK... HE REPLACES PAPERS AND DOCUMENTS IN A DRAWER, SHUTS IT... RISES...

JUSTIN   You kept us going, y'know that? Me and the few of us that got through... Yes, you. When we were down - and God knows, many's the time I was low, ready to throw in the towel - you gave me a kick start...

Your banter, camaraderie, making light of it... To tell you the truth, Xavier, I don't think I'd have made it, only for you...

And then you go and - !.. Oh, Xavier! Xavier! You bloody, bloody fool!.. What sort of suicide is it when you have to live on after doing away with yourself?!

What do you see when you look in the mirror?..

SCENE 36   PRIOR'S OFFICE

PHONE RINGING. MARK LIFTS RECEIVER...

MARK   Hello?.. Oh... you've heard?.. Well, no, it's not looking
                great... No now look Father, you know about as much as I
                do - and that's damn all... Yes, yes of course, 'soon as I
                hear anything definite... Good night, now, Freddie. 'Nite...

MARK CRADLES RECEIVER.

                Ould bags... ringing this hour... 'Couldn't, just couldn't
                hold back... Sniffing... looking for the bit of dirt...

                 And I had Cork and Galway on earlier... If they'd look
                after their own communities!.. Ah-hh.... Every man in the
                Province will have it before much longer. Wouldn't mind
                if it stopped there. But sure, most of them have friends -
                outside... 'Worse than ould ones, some of them...

                Two years, two more years and I'll be back in the ranks...
                Sure who'd want my job, for God's sake?.. Who in his
                right mind would want to be a Prior, this day and age?..

SCENE 37   A CORRIDOR

AIDAN WALKING… CLOAK OVER HABIT… CARRYING
UMBRELLA… FINTAN CATCHES UP WITH HIM.

FINTAN   Aidan?.. Father Aidan!

                AIDAN STOPPING… TURNING…

                Eh, don't mind me asking - but do you have to go out?

AIDAN   What?

FINTAN   It's just, a few of us are up in the Library -

AIDAN   Oh, yes?

FINTAN   Talking about, y'know - Xavier.

AIDAN   Oh-hh.

FINTAN   'Putting our heads together -

AIDAN   Best wait until the Provincial gets back, don't you think?

FINTAN   Ah, it'll do no harm - let off a bit of steam.

AIDAN   Well, tomorrow is my heaviest day, Fintan. I need -

FINTAN   Do. Come up with me. I think you should be in on it.

AIDAN   If - if you reckon I could be of help?

FINTAN   Good man yourself. We'll take the lift - say a prayer to
                the Holy Ghost on the way up…

SCENE 38   THE LIBRARY

BOOKS, BOOKS AND MSS... A GATHERING OF THE BRETHREN...
THE MEETING UNDER WAY AS AIDAN AND FINTAN ENTER,
JOIN THEM...

HUGO	'So far. We haven't put all the bits and pieces together yet.
SENAN	Grim. It's looking grim.
JOHN	Was there ever such a woeful jigsaw?
HUGO	Doesn't sound great, no matter what face you put on it.
GEORGE	Aye, and there's a thing - what face are we going to put on it?
DECLAN	How do you mean?
GEORGE	The people. Out there. His regulars. What are we going to tell them?
HUGO	Huh... Make up a story.
SENAN	We'd have to be all in on it.
JOHN	Together. Stand our ground.
GEORGE	It'll leak for sure.
JOHN	And who'll leak it? Tell me that!
GEORGE	Ochh! There's them in the Community worse than any women.
SENAN	He's right, George's right. God, you can't change your shirt in here but someone knows about it out there.
HUGO	In jig time.
FINTAN	This is different. 'Have to be different.

DECLAN	How will we go about it, so?
HUGO	It'll be up to the Prior. 'Call us together. The whole Community.
JOHN	Y'mean - announce it?
FINTAN	'Make it official, it's the only way.
HUGO	Then swear us to secrecy. Put us under oath if all comes to all.
GEORGE	As sure as God one o' the younger priests'll say it's against the New Theology.
HUGO	The Prior won't be asking them, he'll be telling them.
SENAN	Ho, ho! Good on you, Father! More like old times, that kinda talk!
JOHN	So - what's the story?
HUGO	It'll have to be good - foolproof.
FINTAN	Make it simple. Stick to the basics.
GEORGE	Aye, right. That way we won't get tripped up.
HUGO	Suppose... suppose we say he's gone to England?
JOHN	'Mightn't be much of a lie...
GEORGE	Make it an emergency. A sudden S.O.S. from some Bishop or other.
HUGO	Yeah... Why not? One of his curates got sick - serious, like - and he wired for a replacement.
DECLAN	Will it stick?
SENAN	We'll make it stick.
FINTAN	'Have to work out the details. 'Get the Catholic Directory for England and Wales... 'Name of Diocese, Bishop... A curacy at the back of beyond...
HUGO	Malachy gives a lot of Missions and Retreats over there. He'd surely be able to give us a name and address.

SENAN	That's it!
JOHN	And if the ould ones come to the Mass Office -
DECLAN	They will, they will, nothing surer! -
JOHN	Asking for him -
GEORGE	Wanting to know where he's gone -
SENAN	We can give out a postal address and all!
GEORGE	And if some of them write to him?
JOHN	Ah, they hardly would.
DECLAN	You never know, some of them might chance a few lines.
FINTAN	Any letters could be kept, sent back to the Prior.
SENAN	That's it, then. Let ye do it in the name o' God!..

SCENE 39   GILES... IN HIS ROOM.

GILES

Xavier, huh?.. Not a bad preacher, 'give him his due... 'Could have been out with me, many's the time, if he played his cards right... 'Would have shown him the ropes, marked his card... Ah, but he just sat there, looking at me as if I had two heads...

Well, he's gone now, the Divil riding on his shoulder. Oh, many's the man, many's the man turned away from the plough, went after the fleshpots of Egypt - and lived to rue it... Oh, the folly of it!.. Bitter tears, bitter tears!..

HE MOVES TO A WINDOW, STANDS LOOKING OUT...

Hmmm... Dirty night, no doubt... There they go, droves of them... 'Off buses... crossing over... walking across and around... heading for the Hall... hoping against hope for a full house - or a line atself... Bingo, huh.

Ah, well, sure, it's a night out for them... And all in a good cause: our lads out on the Foreign Missions can't live on air - no more than meself...

SCENE 40   REVERT TO THE LIBRARY

HUGO   You're very quiet there, Father Aidan?..

AIDAN   Eh-hh... No, I was just thinking...

SENAN   Oh yeah?..

AIDAN   There is another way...

DECLAN   Oh? And what might that be, Father?

AIDAN   Tell the truth...

SENAN   Ah, come on, Father!

THEY PROTEST, EXCLAIM... RHURBARB:

JOHN	What!?
GEORGE	Will you have sense, man!
SENAN	Are you going soft in the head or what?
HUGO	Tell the truth - and we still don't know the half of it ourselves!
SENAN	Shock and scandalise half the neighbourhood!
DECLAN	That's it - scandal!
GEORGE	To be avoided at all costs!
JOHN	And no necessity for it -
GEORGE	None in the wide world!..
AIDAN	Are you - finished?
FINTAN	'Might as well drop a bomb while you're at it.
SENAN	It'd be a scandal, Father, the like of, of -
GEORGE	It'd see us all in our graves and still not be died down...
AIDAN	I wonder...
HUGO	Well, you can wonder away. I'm a deal older than you, Aidan, and maybe a bit wiser, and I'm telling you here and now, it'd be the worst scandal to hit this Community ever - ever!
FINTAN	And that's saying something...
AIDAN	Well, just - just suppose we tell it as it is? Give the true picture, as we know it, as much as we -
JOHN	God. Dear God -
AIDAN	Oh, they'd be hurt, the people who come to us. Many of them, doubtless. Hurt, let down, disappointed…
FINTAN	You're avoiding the term.
AIDAN	Very well - scandalised... And then, then the reaction.
DECLAN	What?
AIDAN	In their charity, they would forgive him.

SENAN	Huh…
JOHN	'Don't know about that -
AIDAN	They would say, God love him, anyway, wherever he is, sure he's only human after all…
GEORGE	I wonder?..
AIDAN	And if you don't give them that, Brother George, you have a very poor regard for the people of God.
SENAN	Well, I still say…
AIDAN	But tell them a lie - or a tissue of lies - and if they catch you out, there will be the real hurt, the greater scandal.
JOHN	Hmmm…
AIDAN	A scandal involving the whole Community, not just one.
GEORGE	But that's the whole idea! The cover up will be so exact in every detail -
AIDAN	Oh, dear Lord! Someone was telling me earlier to have sense. Well, I'm trying hard to use the wit God gave me - and it seems to me you have overlooked a vital factor in the equation.
DECLAN	Sorry?
AIDAN	The man himself. Xavier.
FINTAN	What about him?
AIDAN	How do you let him in on this splendid cover-up?..
SENAN	I'm still not with you?
AIDAN	Why, he has only to write to a few friends - make a phone call - telling them where he is, and how…
JOHN	God, yeah -
DECLAN	'Never thought of -
GEORGE	I suppose, aye.
AIDAN	Oh, and while we're at it, there's just one other thing I

	reckon the people out there would do when they heard…
DECLAN	Oh?..
GEORGE	What might that be?
AIDAN	They'd pray for him...
FINTAN	Hmmmm...
SENAN	I wonder…
AIDAN	Oh, yes they would. They'd go on their knees - many of them - and storm Heaven on his behalf...
HUGO	Yes. .. Indeed.
DECLAN	What?..
FINTAN	He's saying, Declan, Father Aidan is saying that if we put out a cock-and-bull story, we'll be denying Xavier the intercession of the Faithful...

SCENE 41   THE MASS OFFICE.

MARK LIFTS THE RECEIVER, DIALS 2,3 DIGITS...
JUSTIN IS NOW IN THE ROOM ASSIGNED TO HIM.
LUGGAGE OPENED... SORTING CLOTHES...
PHONE ON HIS LOCKER RINGS. HE ANSWERS:

JUSTIN	Hello, yes?
MARK	Justin, Mark here -
JUSTIN	Ah, Father Prior! I'm just –

MARK	'You have everything you need?
JUSTIN	Oh, yes, fine -
MARK	Well, you only have to shout... Eh-hh... 'Come across anything in Xavier's room?
JUSTIN	No, nothing that would give us a... Except -
MARK	What?
JUSTIN	'Piece of notepaper. His handwriting. 'Fell out of one of his folders -
MARK	Did you take it with you?
JUSTIN	'Have it right here -
MARK	What's it say?
JUSTIN	'Must be a quotation he came across. Eh-hh. (READING) *"Feed my lambs, feed my sheep... The priest is a shepherd... What does it matter whether he be married or single - as long as he is a good shepherd..."*
MARK	Hmmm... So that's the way he was thinking?
JUSTIN	Well... if he went to the trouble of writing it down?
MARK	Huh. Another piece of the jigsaw... Look, I'm down here in the Mass Office, just locking the safe...
JUSTIN	Ah, ha.
MARK	'Be another few minutes. You go on round to the Community Room when you feel like it, okay?..
JUSTIN	I, I'll just drop into the Choir on the way to say a few -
MARK	Well, say one for me while you're at it -

RECEIVERS REPLACED...

| MARK | Huh... Good Shepherd, how are you!.. 'Fecked off and left |

them... his penitents, regulars... left us to pick up the tab...
Hmmm... Married or single... What does it matter as long
as he is a good..?

Ah-hh-hh! You could mull over that one from now till
Christmas and still not come up with a...

'Long day... And tomorrow?.. Ah, I could do with a
drink...

SCENE 42   AIDAN'S ROOM

HE SITS AT HIS DESK, TYPING SLOWLY, PAINFULLY...
REMINGTON (?) TYPEWRITER... (OF THE PERIOD.)
THEN HE STOPS, ABRUPTLY... STANDS UP...

AIDAN   Ah-hh. .. I can't - concentrate... Too tired now... Tired
               and... Oh, Xavier, Xavier... 'Not that we hit it off all that
               well... I drew back - more often than not - from his, his
               exuberance, spontaneity... And deep down, I suppose - no,
               I know, know I did - I envied him his instant rapport... All
               things to all men... Oh-hh-hh. All I can't, could never be...

'Should go over to Recreation... 'Gesture to Justin. .. 'Put in a, an appearance... 'Don't have to stay... Ah, I dread it... 'Can imagine what they'll be on about...

'Don't have to... It's optional, tonight. . . Justin would understand - no offence - and the Prior. .. I have a heavy day, tomorrow... Still...

My spiritual director says that Recreation - Re-creation - is an important part of Community Life... Staying away, aloof... staying on your own can be a form of self-love - even self-pity... 'disdain for the Community...

And he has, he has a point... And even if he's wrong, even if he's wrong... by following his direction, I cannot lose, spiritually... Then do, do in the name of...

HE MOVES AWAY FROM THE DESK... STOPS.

But if I sit too close to, to… him… I...

Oh, Lord. Oh, dear Lord, purge me...

Mary Immaculate, help me to remain chaste and pure...

SCENE 43   THE COMMUNITY ROOM

THE BRETHREN AT RECREATION, SEATED IN A SEMI-CIRCLE...
SOME JUST ARRIVING... MIMING CONVERSATION... GLASSES...
BOTTLES... WINE, SPIRITS, BEER... ASH TRAYS.

A

MARK	Cheers now, Justin.
JUSTIN	Slainte, Father.
MARK	So... you must be tired after all the travelling?..
JUSTIN	Well, I was when I got to Rome. All in. But the few days there perked me up. No one to disturb me…
MARK	Except the students...
JUSTIN	Ah, Rome is... What can you say? And the College itself is - peaceful. You can almost reach out and touch the past... in the cloister, Library... the Aula Max.
MARK	And they're a grand Community.
JUSTIN	'Got me into a General Audience and all.
MARK	What did you think?
JUSTIN	Hmmm?
MARK	The Pope. How did you find him?
JUSTIN	Oh. 'Looked strained, I thought. A bit fragile. Maybe even - tortured?..
MARK	Ah, well, do y'see, he hasn't the charisma of Pius the Twelfth - he's no Roman aristocrat, Montini. And coming after John the Twenty Third - ah, it was a hard act to follow.
JUSTIN	I, I did hear a rumour...

MARK	Oh-hh?
JUSTIN	It seems he's at work on a new Encyclical. On Marriage, Contraception - all that.
MARK	I see...
JUSTIN	Prepared for him, like.
MARK	But of course...
JUSTIN	But it's a particular School of Theology that's behind this One.
MARK	Conservative?
JUSTIN	Very. Out-and-outers. No two ways about it: any form of artificial contraception will be anathema.
MARK	No room for maneuver?
JUSTIN	None... They say he's seen the first draft or two...
MARK	So?
JUSTIN	The poor man's tormented, whether to sign or not.
MARK	I can imagine - from what I know of him... So when will it be published?
JUSTIN	They say August at the latest.
MARK	Well, if that's the way, it's going to turn a lot of married couples away from the doors down there...
JUSTIN	That's why he's hesitating, they reckon. Some of the Cardinals are pressing him to sign, some are begging him not to...
MARK	Hmmm... Wait and see. Well, I'll tell, Justin: it won't make our job in the Confessional any easier...

B

DECLAN	No word, no?
GEORGE	Xavier?.. No.
GILES	Ah-hh-hh! I have no sympathy for him. None.
JOHN	Some say he's gone to London...
GEORGE	'Only talk, Brother John - no one knows for sure.
GILES	Never did what he was told. Never...
JOHN	If he'd only ring. Someone, anyone. Let us know.
GILES	No man can serves two masters...
GEORGE	'Might be too ashamed...
JOHN	How do you mean?
GEORGE	If he's come to his senses, realised what he's done...
GILES	He who prays will be saved, he who does not pray will be lost -
JOHN	'Must be a terrible way to be -
GILES	Saint Alphonsus. I'm always quoting him -
GEORGE	Ah, we're going round in the dark. No sense in - sure we don't even know whether he's alive or dead or -
GILES	Always on the go. In one door, out the other. When did anyone ever see him on his knees?..
JOHN	If it's true... if he is in London.
GEORGE	What?..
JOHN	And we could contact him.
GILES	What are you on about, Brother? Spill it out.
JOHN	There, there's a priest over there doing great work among the Irish. In the Universe and the Catholic Herald he is, every other week.
GEORGE	Oh, aye. What's this his name is?..
GILES	Casey. Eamonn Casey.

GEORGE	Ah, that's him, that's the man, right enough.
JOHN	Well, what I'm saying is, if we could put him on to Xavier, somehow, he'd do him a power of good - maybe even get him back to us...
GEORGE	Aye... maybe.
GILES	Hmmm... If he's all he's made out to be...

A

MARK	You're lucky in a way that your Archbishop was born in South Africa - they can't touch him.
JUSTIN	Well, I wouldn't go that far. But they could hardly expel him - not like some of the other Churchmen.
MARK	It's a rough regime, no doubt.
JUSTIN	Oh, he's well able for them, the same Archbishop. 'Plays his cards very close to his chest. And they know very well that he doesn't go along with the system...
MARK	Who could?.. Anyway, I'd say he was away a lot - in Rome, like, for the Council?
JUSTIN	Indeed. 'Never missed a session - as far as I know. And I'll say this for him: he did try his best to pass the word down the line, let us know what was happening -
MARK	That's it, that's the thing! If there's no communication from the top where does that leave the likes of us?
JUSTIN	In the dark.
MARK	And we're supposed to be telling the people?!.. Ah, y'know, some of the Bishops we have here are hopeless.

	Hopeless! 'Haven't a word for a dog. You'd need a tin opener to get anything out of them...
JUSTIN	And your own man here in Dublin - did he open up at all under the Roman sun?
MARK	Well, if he did atself, he certainly closed up again when he got back to base.
JUSTIN	'Just the same?
MARK	I don't think he'll ever be any different. Distant, y'know. Removed. Cold you might say - if you didn't know him. And I'm one of the many that don't know him. 'Could be a saint for all I know. Certainly, an intellectual. But a man of the people? I doubt it, somehow... Still, we have to live with it: Archbishop of Dublin by the grace of God -
JUSTIN	And the active influence of de Valera.
MARK	Well, you can say that as a visitor. Me, I'll keep my counsel...
JUSTIN	Any sign of him lifting the ban on Trinity College?
MARK	Not a hope - it's still a mortlar... I'll say this much for him, though: when he was out in Rome, up every morning, said his prayers, Office, did his meditation before Mass - while some of them were still sleeping off the night before.
JUSTIN	Hmmm... So how do his own clergy get on with him?
MARK	Some didn't go along with his appointment. But then some of them wouldn't go along with any appointment.
JUSTIN	Sure, what could they do? Roma locuta est...
MARK	Indeed. And the Papal Nuncio wasn't exactly pulling names out of a hat. There's a thing, though...
JUSTIN	Hmmm?

MARK	They say with his own priests, he's the milk of human kindness if one of them goes off the rails, gets into any kind of female trouble.
JUSTIN	'One up for John Charles.
MARK	But an unfortunate curate, somewhere, or a parish priest - doing his best - if he puts a foot wrong, McQuaid will come down on him like a ton of bricks. Peculiar, isn't it?..
JUSTIN	Indeed... So Xavier would be well got if he showed up at the Palace?
MARK	Oh-hh! Received with open arms!..

C

FINTAN	Looks like Leonard will have to think again...
HUGO	Indeed. He'll have a fit when he hears...
SENAN	How do y'mean, Father?
FINTAN	Well, he's Director of Missions and Retreats -
HUGO	'Had Xavier down for two in Lent -
FINTAN	One in Navan with Columbanus and Ultan -
HUGO	And the other in the Curragh.
SENAN	The Army, huh?
FINTAN	Yeah. A big one, that -
HUGO	That's why Leonard was sending his best troops.
FINTAN	Now he'll just have to look around, see who's available.
HUGO	'Always a problem, every year.
SENAN	Sorry, I'm not with you, Father?
HUGO	Lent's a busy time, Senan. 'Hard enough to get a Prior to

	release a man for a fortnight -
FINTAN	Never mind a month.
SENAN	He'll be missed, huh? Father Xavier.
FINTAN	Sorely. And in more ways that one.
HUGO	Always in great demand. Sometimes I felt a twinge of envy, he was so popular.
FINTAN	You're not the only one...
SENAN	Were you ever out with him, Father?
HUGO	About two years ago was the last. Dominic and meself. Dolphin's Barn. Xavier was down the road in Fatima.
FINTAN	'Strong team, that.
HUGO	Well, whatever about us, he was a great man to go. 'Looked the part and certainly sounded the part.
FINTAN	'Them hanging on his every word -
HUGO	You could hear a pin drop -
SENAN	Be gor, huh...
HUGO	And he'd stay in the Confessional for hours on end - as long as there was a sinner kneeling outside, a soul to be saved.
FINTAN	A lion in the pulpit, a lamb in the box...
SENAN	You'd be proud of him, huh?
HUGO	How could you not be?! -
FINTAN	One of our own, doing great work for the Church -
SENAN	Be dad!
HUGO	And do y'know, at table with the Parish Priest and the curates, he'd hold his own - manners, conversation... You could depend on him.
SENAN	Never let himself down, huh?
FINTAN	Nor us...

HUGO	And as likely as not one of the curates, over coffee, would say to him - "Will you tell us that joke, Father? - What joke? - Ah, y'know, the one you told from the pulpit the other night. The people loved it - and I know the P.P. would love it, too..." And he would, he would...
SENAN	Ah, what got into him at all, at all?
FINTAN	Don't know, I do not know...
SENAN	'Could have had a great life.
HUGO	The world at his feet - and he goes and kicks it away.

A

MARK	And our own Sean Lemass, eh. God, he was a great Taoiseach.
JUSTIN	Indeed...
MARK	So what did you think of him going up to Belfast there a while back to meet O'Neill? At Stormont, no less.
JUSTIN	Wonders will never cease. Not that it caused much of a ripple out where I am.
MARK	The grand gesture and a hard head for business – that was Lemass for you.
JUSTIN	Did anything come of it?
MARK	No, nor won't. It'll fizzle out.
JUSTIN	Do you not think it might be a, a beginning -
MARK:	No chance. They're too set in their ways - entrenched. "No Surrender." It'll always be the same up there.

JUSTIN	Yeah, I suppose...
MARK	I never go across the Border myself unless I have to. Different breed. Race apart. Ah, let them at it, that's what I say. Who'd want them? God! Can you imagine? Talk about wasting your honey on the desert air! I'll tell you, Justin, you're far better off where you are: at least you have some hope of converting the blacks...
JUSTIN	Ah, come on now, Father. It can't be as grim as -
MARK	Grim?!.. There's as much hope, now, of ending Partition as there is of doing away with Apartheid in South Africa... And you can't get much grimmer than that, now can you?
JUSTIN	Well... we can only hope. Things are beginning to change - look at America.
MARK	There'll be no Civil Rights in the Six Counties. Never. And if the Nationalists ever attempted a Civil Rights March - be god, they'd be massacred!
JUSTIN	That's what they said about the Deep South - and now look what's happening.
MARK	Yeah, well we don't have a Martin Luther King - and no sign of one appearing...
JUSTIN	I wouldn't mind but we're all one country - at least, geograph -
MARK	We were never one nation, Father - and never will be...

SCENE 44   EMMANUEL'ROOM

EMMANUEL IN SOME DISTRESS, LYING HALF IN, HALF OUT OF
BED. OCCASIONAL LIGHTS.

MANUEL   Oh - hh - hhh… Brother?.. Br-Brother?.. Are you?.. Where
              are you?.. Brother?.. Brother John?.. Help… I need…
              John?.. any… any… Ah-hhh…

SCENE 45   THE COMMUNITY ROOM

THE BRETHREN, DRINKING… TALKATIVE – EXPANSIVE…

B and C

HUGO   … No, not at all. 'Didn't do well in his exams. Ever.
DECLAN   'Wasn't a scholar, so?
HUGO   Hardly. Would you go along with that, Fintan?
FINTAN   Well, from what I know, he was a student all right - but off
              the course.
GILES   "And may they be cursed who by their bad example…"
JOHN   (TO FINTAN) How do y'mean, Father?
FINTAN   'Read up and down, over and back - anything, everything,
              that took his fancy.

92

DECLAN	Except what he was supposed to be - ?
FINTAN	Now you have it. The rest of them slogging away at the Curriculum and he'd be up on the roof - or over in the Library - reading, dreaming -
HUGO	Up on the ladder, maybe, sniffing at some musty manuscript.
GILES	"… tear down and bring to ruin what you build up…"
JOHN	So how did he manage when it came to, to -
HUGO	Exams?
FINTAN	That's just it, he didn't. Not in Rome, anyway. 'Scraped through his orals. Six out of ten was about as much as he ever could manage -
HUGO	A misericordia pass, nearly every time.
FINTAN	Useless at Latin - though he could take the Italians off to a T…
FINTAN	A born mimic.
HUGO	And yet he got the gist of it, somehow.
GILES	"… and do not cease to build up through the holy brethren of this order…"
FINTAN	As a matter of fact... Maybe I shouldn't say this...
JOHN	What, Father? What?
FINTAN	There was a question mark over him, as far as I know.
DECLAN	How do y'mean, Father?..
FINTAN	Whether to let him go on for Ordination or not...
JOHN	Oh-hh...
DECLAN	Was that the way?..
HUGO	'Not easy to send a man packing unless he makes the first move himself.
JOHN	And Xavier himself, like, didn't have any doubts?..

HUGO	If he had he kept them to himself -
FINTAN	Oh, no. No, he wanted to go through. 'Told the Student Master he knew what he was doing. 'Assured him...
SENAN	That would have been - ?
HUGO	Cornelius. He's in Waterford now.
FINTAN	So what was he to do? He could see the good in Xavier, the talent. And he couldn't fault him when it came to prayer, meditation...
HUGO	'Reckoned he'd come to no harm in a Priory down the country.
GEORGE	So even as a student he was what you might call unusual?
HUGO	Unusual? He was a rare specimen!
FINTAN	And wild into the bargain. Even then. God, you wouldn't know what he'd get up to next!
GEORGE	Oh-hh?..
GILES	The habit doesn't make the friar.
FINTAN	Like... (CHUCKLING) God, yeah...
DECLAN	What, Father? Tell us.
HUGO	Come on, Fintan. Share it.
FINTAN	Ha, ha... Saint Patrick's Day...
JOHN	What about it?
FINTAN	Well, you know yourself, it's the biggest day of the year we have in Rome.
GEORGE	Yes, yes?!
DECLAN	I was there for it myself one year. My Jubilee.
FINTAN	The College crowded, the Church packed. Visitors and guests and all like that -
HUGO	And the sun shining, no doubt - not like the misery we go through here.

FINTAN	Well, anyway. It's the custom - two or three hostesses from Aer Lingus standing at the top of the steps -
HUGO	In their uniforms -
FINTAN	Greeting people as they arrived, pinning shamrock on them before they went on into the Church -
HUGO	Oh, lovely looking. Irish coleens in their prime. Lovely, entirely.
DECLAN	Oh, dear. Dear, dear, dear.
HUGO	About as near as we got to a young one over the four years we were there.
JOHN	Ahem. Ahem.
GILES	From the snares of the Evil One, oh Lord, deliver us…
SENAN	Well, what? What!
FINTAN	Xavier takes his place in the queue.
JOHN	Yeah? Yeah!
FINTAN	And when his turn comes he steps forward, says hello and how are you, and the air hostess pins a sprig of shamrock on the tunic of his habit...
SENAN	So?.
FINTAN	Ha!
DECLAN	What? What, Father?
FINTAN	He goes round a corner, takes down the shamrock - and away back round with him to the end of the queue!
JOHN	He didn't - what?!
DECLAN	Never! Are you joking?
HUGO	Be God, I wouldn't put it past him!
FINTAN	I'm telling you - not the word of a lie.
SENAN	Well, well, well - huh?
FINTAN	It was Benignus told me - he was there, saw it -

HUGO: That'd be him all right - that'd be Xavier!

AD-LIBBING... SPONTANEOUS LAUGHTER...

A

MARK   John F. Kennedy, huh.

JUSTIN   There'll never be his like...

MARK   'Not one of us doesn't know where he was and what he
            was doing when the news started coming in from Dallas.

JUSTIN   Just goes to show you, the esteem he was -

MARK   Oh, what!? 'Great man, great President. And a very devout
            Catholic - no matter what the pressures of office. I have it
            for a fact, Justin, he was at Mass and Communion that
            morning before he set out in the motorcade. Now. There's
            one for you...

JUSTIN   Hmmm... And when he came to Ireland -

MARK   You missed it! The people worshipped him, turned out in
            their thousands!

JUSTIN   'Had to be something else -

MARK   I was in Wexford, y'know, when he passed through,
            waving from the car. And as near to him as I am to you
            now on the platform when he gave the speech down the
            Quays.

JUSTIN   You could never forget a -

MARK   Oh, I'm telling you!.. There was a man among men, a
            leader, a god - God forgive me... And here, didn't the
            Bishop of Ferns take a turn and pass away of a sudden?..

JUSTIN   'Didn't know that -

MARK	'Kept hush-hush until the President was well on his way.
JUSTIN	Oh?..
MARK	'Safact... Poor Doctor Staunton, a good man in many ways. Well, sure, we buried him as best we could but the timing was all wrong. 'Bit of an anti-climax, if you know what I mean...
JUSTIN	Yes, I -
MARK	And now Bobby on his way to the White House, nothing to stop him. Mark my words, Justin, we haven't seen the last of the Kennedy clan - not by a long shot...

OUTBURST OF LAUGHTER FROM THE BRETHREN...

JUSTIN	Ha! The lads are moving into top gear -
MARK	Here, what was that, huh? Did we miss a good one?
JUSTIN	Are you entertaining the troops, Senan?
GILES	He's in good form right enough, Prior -
MARK	Come on, Brother, let us in on it -
SENAN	Ah, 'twas nothing, Father, just an ould chestnut -
MARK	No, now you're not getting off that light, sometimes the old ones are the best -
DECLAN	Sure you heard it before long since, Father.
GEORGE	'Didn't find it all that funny -
MARK	Come on, Senan, give us all a laugh. God knows we could do with one...
SENAN	Ah, it's just, about Doctor Browne, the Bishop of Galway -
MARK	What about him? -
SENAN	Well, he was walking along Salthill with his secretary one summer's day -

HUGO	Keeping his eyes down, no doubt!

RHURBARB FROM THE BRETHREN: HO, HO! HA, HA! AH, NOW!

SENAN	Well, what do y'know but doesn't he spot this cleric down on the rocks smoking a great big cigar.
DECLAN	Oh-hh. Oh, what!
FINTAN	Trouble. Trouble on the horizon -
MARK	Whist will ye, let him finish the story!
SENAN	So Doctor Browne sends his secretary over with the message: Michael of Galway does not approve of clerics smoking in public -
GILES	Ah ha! That was telling him!
SENAN	Back comes the secretary: he says to tell you, m'Lord - Daniel of Baltimore doesn't mind at all!

LAUGHTER AND ADLIBBING FROM THE BRETHREN

- Good on you, Brother! -

- That's good all right! –

- 'Love to have seen his face! -

- You never lost it, Senan! -

- Where does he get them?! - etc.

BROTHER JOHN SLIPS AWAY... EXITS.

MARK	Well, well, well -
JUSTIN	I'll take that one back with me to Jo'burg –

GILES   Would you be bothered?

FINTAN   I'd say the Bishop's nose got even longer! -

HUGO   Im - ha, ha - impossible! Ha, ha -

SENAN   Ah, you heard it before, Father Prior, must have -

MARK   Well, and if I did atself, I'm not saying... What I will say is
            this, if I can have your ear for a minute...

ADLIBBING, CHUCKLING SUBSIDES... SOME COUGHING...

            It's just - one or two worries I'd like to share with ye...
            And I know, full well, that ye've been worrying about the
            very same things...
            Anyway. Emmanuel comes to mind. We all know he's
            going downhill. Indeed, we're reaching the stage where
            we'll no longer be able to cope with him here in the
            Community...

COUGHING... QUIET MURMURING...

            I don't want any of ye, priest or brother, to approach him
            for Confession from now on. Is that understood?

MURMURS OF ASSENT...

            Let ye pass the word on to those who didn't make it into
            Recreation tonight - for one reason or another...

            Now. As regards Xavier... I'm as worried - and as upset -

as any of ye... Maybe more than most: I was his Superior; he was in my charge... At this moment in time, I haven't a clue where he is - and that's no word of a lie...

All the signs point to a planned, premeditated exit. It looks like he has taken off - deliberately... We think of London, almost at once. But we just don't know...

Anyway, I'll keep you posted, as best I can.

And look: Father Provincial will be back with us before much longer. He is, of course, aware of the situation; we are in constant touch by 'phone... So it's out of my hands, really this is one for the Man Himself - and his Definitors...

UNCOMFORTABLE MURMURS... COUGHING...

And in the case of Emmanuel, they may well decide the time has come to transfer him to a Nursing Home...

For his own sake. His own very best good. Where he will be looked after, professionally, nursed competently, to the end of his days...
Now that's in no way intended to take one iota from the trojan work Brother John has been doing over the last -

MURMURS OF ASSENT...

	Where is he, anyway?
GILES	Here a minute ago -
GEORGE	He just slipped out to check on, on -
MARK	Emmanuel? There, y'see? That's my point, exactly.
GILES	The poor man can't even relax at Recreation -

HUGO	(ASIDE) Not like yourself, Giles...
GILES	(ASIDE... PETULANT) What's that supposed to mean?

MARK   Eh-hh, as you know, we all went into Health Insurance on a group scheme some years ago. Emmanuel was far too old to qualify. So we'll have to bear the full cost of a Nursing Home if and when it happens. But God's good, we'll manage, somehow... Now... that's enough out of me, I'll just slip away… see to a few…

ADLIBBING AS MARK EXITS:

"Good night, Prior... Sleep well, Father... Thank you, Mark... God bless..." etc.

THE BRETHREN SETTLE DOWN AGAIN... DRINKS POURED...

GILES	Tell us, anyway. The Prior didn't say anything else to you about..?
JUSTIN	Xavier? No.
GILES	Out of the corner of his mouth, like? -
JUSTIN	What the Prior said just now, Giles, was straight up, no messing.

FINTAN	You can believe it...
DECLAN	Ah, the poor man, sure he has his hands full -
GEORGE	If he was on a salary he'd be earning great money.
HUGO	It's no joke...
FINTAN	Well, if you take the Prior and multiply by a hundred you'll have some idea what the Provincial has on his plate.
DECLAN	They all need our prayers and no doubt about it -
SENAN	Ah, this is desperate, dismal - you'd swear we were all on gin!
GEORGE	What's eating you now, Senan?
SENAN	Is it Recreation or is it not - I ask ye? Come on, someone liven it up!
HUGO	'Better send for Aidan, so - to recite one of his poems!

HALF HEARTED LAUGHTER... SUBSIDING...

SENAN	Ah, we can do better than that! It's years now since Father Justin gave us a song!
GILES	Are you mad? This hour! -
FINTAN	Will you give the man a chance?! -
HUGO	Sure he's only finding his feet!
SENAN	Do, Father, do! Give us all a lift!
GEORGE	Senan, Senan, are you losing the run of yourself? -
SENAN	Give us "Mary Anne" - the way only you can sing it!
DECLAN	And wake all the others?!
SENAN	"Mary Anne" - and we'll all join in on the chorus!
GILES	Is the whiskey gone to your head, Brother - or what?
SENAN	Come on, Father - will I start you off? (SINGING) "Oh-oh, Mary, and do you remember... "

A FEW BARS OF 'MARY ANNE...' (VIDE ADDENDUM.)

FINTAN   That's enough, Senan -

HUGO Shussschhh, will you?! -

JUSTIN   Another night, Brother, I'd be happy to -

SENAN   Ah, Father! You're lettin' us down -

HUGO   (ASIDE) Senan! Will you for God's sake have a bit of
            cop-on?!

SENAN   Huh? What? -

HUGO   (INDICATING THE HOUSE GUEST) Justin...

SENAN   Oh-hh?.. Oh, sorry, Father, I -

JOHN HEARD OFF, CALLING. DOOR BURSTS OPEN.

JOHN   Quick! Come quick! -

DECLAN   Jesus, Mary and -

HUGO   Emmanuel? -

JOHN   I think he's -

FINTAN   Quick! Move it! -

CHAIRS MOVED... A TUMBLER OVERTURNED...

JOHN   Is the Prior not here?

FINTAN   'Round to the Oratory, Hugo - get the oils!

HUGO   (GOING) There now -

SENAN   Ah, Holy God!

FINTAN   Out of my way, George!

GEORGE	Aye, right, right -
GILES	Is there any sign of life - or is he gone altogether?
HUGO	Declan, call the Prior, tell him -
DECLAN	Oh, yes! Yes, I -
FINTAN	George, ring for the doctor -
GEORGE	His number? –
FINTAN	On the notice board -
DECLAN	Jesus, Mary and Joseph, assist us now and in our -

RHURBARB AS THEY MAKE A HASTY EXIT...

GILES CROSSES TOWARDS JUSTIN.

GILES	'Didn't say. Brother John didn't say...
JUSTIN	'Didn't hear you. 'Poor man's in shock.
GILES	Yeah, I suppose... Anyway. Maybe it's God's turn now...
JUSTIN	Sorry?
GILES	To look after Emmanuel. We had him long enough...
JUSTIN	Oh. Oh-hh-hh...

GILES LIFTS A BOTTLE, POURS FOR JUSTIN AND HIMSELF.

	God, Giles, what are you doing?
GILES	Topping you up - what do you think I'm doing?
JUSTIN	But I mean, I mean -
GILES	Lookit here to me, Justin, if he's gone, he's gone - and Fintan's anointing him this minute. All as it should be. No point in crowding into the room to gawk at him - do y'follow?

JUSTIN	Eh-hh. I -
GILES	It'd be different if it was out in the Bush and you maybe the only priest for miles...
JUSTIN	Of course, yes. Still, I -
GILES	Cheers, now. Slainte.
JUSTIN	Ah, God, Giles, this isn't on! I mean, where's your sense of, of fraternity?
GILES	Fraternity? Sure isn't this what it's all about?! If our brother in Christ is on the way to his eternal reward, the least we can do is wish him bon voyage!
JUSTIN	Oh, I... I don't know -
GILES	He persevered to the end – he's saved. Was there ever a greater cause for fraternal rejoicing - I ask you?
JUSTIN	Oh... no disputing that. It's just -
GILES	Stepping into the Garden of Paradise he is this minute, Emmanuel... all sweetness and light, serenity and peace, in saecula saeculorum... But as for your other man…
JUSTIN	What?
GILES	How will it go for him at the Final Reckoning?
JUSTIN	Xavier?
GILES	'Put his hand to the plough and looked back... turned away from the Cross to wallow in the flesh pots of Egypt.
JUSTIN	Ah, Giles! For God's sake!
GILES	"Depart from me, ye cursed, into everlasting fire... Better for that man if he had never been born – "
JUSTIN	Shame on you! Sitting there, nursing a whiskey, judging a fellow priest!
GILES	Don't have to - he's judged himself!
JUSTIN	We'll leave that to God, if you don't mind - and he

	happens to be a God of infinite mercy and forgiveness!
GILES	Oh yes, sure, no doubt. But will Xavier be able to forgive himself? Hmmm? Huh?.. Now. There's one for you.
JUSTIN	'Only has to look at Christ on the Cross, arms extended -
GILES	Oh, Father, Father! When he comes to the end of his days? Will he sink into the depths of despair, end an abject existence, maybe, in soul-searing remorse?..
JUSTIN	In the name of - ! What School of Theology did you go to?!
GILES	Ah, you can say what you like: I still wouldn't want to be in his shoes when my time is up. Oh, no, no way...

JUSTIN SETS DOWN HIS DRINK, MAKES TO STAND...

JUSTIN	I, I think, if you'll excuse me - I want to -
GILES	Are you not going to wait for the others?
JUSTIN	What?
GILES	They'll be back over. Any minute now. Some of them, anyhow...
JUSTIN	Back? Here?..
GILES :	It'll be for the Prior to make the final arrangements...
JUSTIN	But why? I mean, why would they come back here?
GILES	For a drink - what else?.. 'Lend each other a bit of support, the few of us that are left... 'Strength in numbers, eh?
JUSTIN	Hmmm... Well, I -
GILES	Anyway, most of them will have sobered up by now: not every night in the year they see a fellow traveller passing on... the Prior closing his eyes.
JUSTIN	I, I'll just go round, see if I can be of any -

GILES	Ah, sure, wasn't I a Prior meself in the good old days? A stint here, a term there... one house or another. Well I know the score. Anthony, Walter, Athanasius, Humilis - oh, many's the man I buried.
JUSTIN	Yes, well, I -
GILES	Hard times, Father, hard times. But we were happy. Didn't know any differ...
JUSTIN	Indeed -
GILES	And there's a thing, Justin. I ruled with a firm hand but an even one. My Community knew where they stood - they played fair with me, I played fair with them. But if one of them stepped out of line..!
JUSTIN	I can imagine -
GILES	And I'll tell you: if I was Xavier's Superior he'd still be in - not out there, God knows where!
JUSTIN	You reckon?..
GILES	I know!.. Be God, I'd have sat on him! 'Given far too much slack, he was - far, far too much leeway... Sure half the time no one knew where he was or what he was at - if he knew himself.
JUSTIN	Well, maybe he was -
GILES	Not showing up for Divine Office or Meditation... Sleeping it out when he was on an early Mass - or down for supply in a neighbouring Parish... Taking the car when it was needed for sick calls.
JUSTIN	Are you, are you finished?..
GILES	And Mark, God love him, anyhow, the craethur, covering for him more often than not! And the Pro himself!? Huh?

	The blind eye and the deaf ear! When a flyin' kick in the arse would have done the whelp a world of good, brought him to heel! –
JUSTIN	Or broken his spirit? -
GILES	Ah, bullshit - if you'll pardon the expression...
JUSTIN	I'll try -
GILES	All this business about giving a man enough rope and he'll hang himself?! Nonsense! Put a rope round him and give it a good chuck ever so often - that's what I say!..
JUSTIN	'Puppet on a string -
GILES	Obedience, Father, Obedience! That's what's needed, more than ever, in the Church today - and leave debate to Democracy!
JUSTIN	So no discussion, no argument - yes sir, no sir, three bags full -
GILES	Lookit here to me: Christ founded the Church, right? If he wanted a Democracy He would have made it a Democracy. But he didn't. So what you have is a Hierarchy. The orders come down from the top, that's how it is and that's how it should be. Ours not to reason why...
JUSTIN	They wouldn't agree with you...
GILES	Who?
JUSTIN	The Fathers of the Second Vatican Council.
GILES	Huh!
JUSTIN	Times have changed, Father -
GILES	The Ten Commandments haven't changed - nor will they ever! No nor the Holy Rule of our Order!..
JUSTIN	You're not preaching at me, by any chance?
GILES	Oh, you can scoff all you want, I stand by the old order -

the way it was, the way it should be. Sin is sin. Give it a fancy name if you want - but fornication is fornication, adultery is adultery!

JUSTIN   Black is black, white white - and no greys.

GILES   No nonsense! And there's too much of that around here, too much - laxity!

JUSTIN   God, don't let them hear you saying -

GILES   'No talk these days of the fear o' God. Well, it was, is, and always will be the beginning of Wisdom!...

JUSTIN   Are you eh, sure you haven't had enough for one night?

GILES   Huh! Don't talk to me about drink, Justin. Talk to your friend. When you track him down...

JUSTIN   Yes, I - I must admit I have been told a few -

GILES   Well, you were told right!

JUSTIN   He, he was hitting it?

GILES   Oh, what!

JUSTIN   'That bad?..

GILES   Father, I saw him, watched him... the Big Dinner on a Feast Day... up here that night... lettin' it back... 'No favours, 'did himself no favours...

JUSTIN   'Man takes the bottle, the bottle takes the man.

GILES   You could see the change in him - I could, anyhow -

JUSTIN   Like?..

GILES   Ah-hh... He'd be in great form at first - laughing, joking - more often than not at someone else's expense -

JUSTIN   Ha. That I do know!

GILES   And then, of a sudden, he'd round on one of us, light on something that was said, pick an argument - 'nights he even started a row... 'Nice fella, how are ya! When he got into that mood there was nothing nice about him.

JUSTIN   Deadly.

GILES   Oh, it was on the tip of my tongue - more than once -
to say it to him.

JUSTIN   Not easy - maybe do more harm than good…

GILES   Well, like... if it's a priest or a brother that's stepping out
of line, that's one thing. But if it's a Superior? A Prior say,
or a Provincial - maybe a Bishop?

JUSTIN   Harder still -

GILES   Harder? It's bloodywell near impossible! What do you do?
What can anyone do?

JUSTIN   I know, yes -

GILES   And fear hanging over every last one of us! Ah, I'll tell
you, Justin, it'd be the brave curate or parish priest that'd
take on his Bishop, 'this day and age.

JUSTIN   Maybe get a belt of a crozier -

GILES   "My Lord, I'm sorry to have to tell you but your drinking
and high living is the talk of the Diocese. You're giving
grave scandal to the people. 'Need to go way somewhere
to dry out, get treatment. We'll cover for you..."

JUSTIN   Just like that, huh?

GILES   Can you imagine? The answer he'd get?

JUSTIN   What'll it be - a drink or a transfer?

GILES   I'd say there'd be total denial. And a severe reprimand -
"How dare you even suggest..?!" But do y'see what I
mean, what I'm getting at?..

JUSTIN   Who minds the minder?

GILES   Exactly! Now you have it. In a nutshell… But it'll be a
sober Xavier you'll be meeting when the time comes.

JUSTIN	What? I'm not with you? -
GILES	When he breaks cover as he surely must, sooner or later - and you go to meet him…
JUSTIN	Well, I - Wild horses wouldn't stop me. That's if he'll want me to -
GILES	Oh, he will, I'll take bets on it... And you'll find him embarrassed, surely - nervous, defensive, guilty, maybe even the bit of remorse -
JUSTIN	And he'll find me - fraternal. No judgement, much less condemnation -
GILES	Indeed. All as it should be... And you'll give him the gist of what we were at this night...
JUSTIN	(HESITANT) Eh-hh..?
GILES	You will, you will. Xavier, says you, Giles sends his warmest regards and sincerest best wishes…
	And he says to tell you, you wouldn't be in the fix you're in today if he'd been Prior…
	that you'd still be here, doing great work for the Glory of God and His Church...
	that there was nothing a sizzling kick in the arse wouldn't have sorted out...
	Now. Will you remember that?
JUSTIN	(DRILY) How could I possibly forget?..

DOOR... VOICES OFF, APPROACHING...

END OF ACT ONE

ACT TWO

SCENE 46   THE CHURCH

Quite crowded. Some women still scarved… Some nuns/Religious still in their habits/head gear…

The community assembled in and around the sanctuary, High altar.

Fr Jarlath, Minister Provincial, chief celebrant at Emmanuel's requiem mass, is assisted by Fathers Fintan and Aidan - deacon and subdeacon - robed in black vestments. They face towards the congregation.

A number of friars begin to sing, unaccompanied, ***Dies Ira, Dies Irae...*** Sung well, as a choral, this passage of Gregorian chant is quite riveting.

A number of friars (6?) enter at the back of the church, shouldering a coffin, and move slowly down along the centre aisle and up unto the sanctuary... finally placing the coffin in position, to one side.

As the chant ends, Jarlath begins to address the congregation:

JARLATH   My dear brethren... We have come together this morning on this sad-joyous, joyous-sad, occasion... to pay a last, fond, final farewell to a dear, revered member of this community: Father Emmanuel.

To many of you who are daily Mass-goers in this church he was a frail figure – snow-white hair, reddish complexion, stooped – who quietly said Mass on one of the side altars... then returned to the cloister...

Back to the quiet of his room... to his books, papers, documents, files... All his long life, Emmanuel was a student, a scholar, a man of letters... Study, research, sharing his findings with others in one academic publication or another - that was his apostolate… way of life... his vocation...

SCENE 47   THE KITCHEN

A FUSSING, BUSTLING BROTHER SENAN AT THE AGA COOKER: POTS, PANS... PREPARING A MEAL FOR THE COMMUNITY AND VISITNG FRIARS... TAKING IT IN HIS STRIDE FOR ALL THAT... SINGING RANDOM SNATCHES OF "MARY ANNE" AS HE WORKS AWAY...

SENAN   "Put more turf on the fire, Mary Anne... for the weather is dreary and cold... Slap down an ould sod, Mary Anne…"

HE TURNS AWAY FROM THE COOKER TOWARD A LARGE UNIT, CENTRE, USED FOR CARVING, ETC. A STACK OF PLATES AT ONE END. HE BEGINS TO PLACE PLATES SIDE BY SIDE ACROSS THIS SERVING AREA...

"… for we're both grown weary and old..."

Hmmmm... Smoked salmon... Huh... 'Tis far from smoked salmon we were reared...

HE CROSSES TO THE FRIDGE, OPENS IT, REACHES IN, TAKES OUT TWO, THREE "SIDES OF SMOKED SALMON..." "AND WE'LL TALK OF OLD TIMES…" AS HE CROSSES BACK TO THE UNIT.

And as sure as God one of them'll sidle up to me, drop it in me ear - "Fish doesn't agree with me, Brother." Aye, well... he can twiddle his thumbs for all I care, do the crossword, while the rest of them are digging into the extra course!

"Oh-oh, Mary my dear, be of good cheer and slap down an ould sod on the fire..."

SCENE 48   THE CHURCH

JARLATH   His reputation as a scholar and historian went before him. His name was well known in the great universities of Europe. None more so than in his beloved Prague - old Prague as he often referred to the city of his choice. Right to the very end, Prague remained the place that held for him the happiest memories...

SCENE 49   THE KITCHEN

SENAN BUSTLING AS BEFORE... SINGING...

"Oh, me name it is Patsy Maloney... from the hilltops near Mullinacrew..."

Boiled... mashed... baked... Spuds and more spuds... Aye, and carrots and turnips in a puree... Be God, I'll tell you, it's far from puree we were reared...

"I'm in love with a sweet little coleen... and I hope soon to make her my own..."

HE BREAKS OFF AS A THOUGHT OCCURS TO HIM:

How many of them will go on to the grave, I wonder?.. Ha!.. As soon as he's hearsed they'll be back in lively... grubbing, letting it back... Then away again to catch an early... Amiens street... Westland Row... Kingsbridge... Back to the nest...

And the brothers'll clear up, clean up, stack the dish washer, bin the empties... and shut up…

"She lives with her father and mother... And wherever in life I may wander... I think of that darlin' spot still..."

SCENE 50   **THE CHURCH.**

JARLATH   For all his undisputed scholarship, Emmanuel was a man of deep faith and humility. A man of prayer. First into choir in his younger years before age began to catch up with him - he was an example to us all.

And it is this aspect of his life that I wish to put before you, my dear brethren, this morning... Emmanuel is as much as saying to us: Pray... Without deep, personal prayer we are empty, weak, vessels of clay... Prayer is the powerhouse, the source of our spiritual strength...

SCENE 51   **THE KITCHEN**

SENAN   "And we'll talk of ould times, Mary Ann... and the troubles of life we've been through..."

ENTER IN HASTE DECLAN, JOHN, GEORGE...

GEORGE   Ah, there you're, old stock -

JOHN   How is it coming, Senan? -

DECLAN   God bless us, the heat!

SENAN   And getting hotter be the minute! Brother cook, I'll have
            yis know, has only the one pair of hands!

DECLAN   Six more now, Senan -

SENAN   Right shower y'are, showing up at the final fence!

HE POINTS TO A SELECTION OF WINE BOTTLES.

            Twelve red and the same white. George, will you do the
            needful?

GEORGE: No sooner said than -

GEORGE PICKS UP A CORK SCREW...

SENAN   Will you keep an eye on the veg, Declan? I'd say they're
            nearly -

DECLAN   Will do -

SENAN   Oh, and John. The lamb should be well done by now -

JOHN   Do you want me to start carving? -

SENAN   Is it nearly over?

GEORGE   Just about. The Pro is starting the last salute -

SENAN   Get a move on, so... Do you know how to make gravy,
            John?

JOHN   Haven't a clue -

SENAN   Come 'er to me. About fizzin' time you learnt!..

SCENE 52   THE CHURCH

JARLATH TAKES A SPRINKLER FROM A SERVER/FRIAR...
BEGINS TO MOVE AROUND THE COFFIN, SPRINKLING "HOLY
WATER..."

THEN HE SPOONS INCENSE INTO A THURIBLE, TAKES IT FROM
A SERVER/FRIAR... WALKS AROUND THE COFFIN SWINGING
THE THURIBLE.

EVEN AS HE DOES SO, THE GROUP OF FRIARS (EXTRAS) THAT
MAKE UP THE CHOIR BEGIN TO SING **IN PARADISUM**... AGAIN,
A STIRRING PIECE OF GREGORIAN CHANT WHEN SUNG WELL,
UNACCOMPANIED...

> "In paradisum deducant te Angeli;
> in tuo adventu suscipiant te Martyres
> et perducant te in civitatem sanctam Jerusalem.
> Chorus Angelorum te suscipiat,
> et cum Lazaro quondam paupere aeternam habeas requiem."

AT THE SAME TIME, THE SIX FRIARS WHO CARRIED THE
COFFIN AT THE BEGINNING OF THE SCENE NOW LIFT IT
SHOULDER HIGH... TURN TOWARDS THE CONGREGATION...

SCENE 52   THE PRIOR'S OFFICE.

A DEJECTED MARK ENTERS, CLOSING THE DOOR BEHIND HIM, ABRUPTLY.

HE THROWS HIS KEYS ON THE DESK... BEGINS TO MOVE AROUND THE ROOM... ANNOYED... BROKEN MONOLOGUE...

MARK   'Last o' them gone... 'Can't wait to get back - to report... Looking at me as if I had two heads, some of them.

I'm a prior, damnit - not a jailer!..

I have a big community here - how am I supposed to...?

'Bent on blood, eh?.. Moved at the next chapter... Me, for sure... Huh...

I won't be sorry... Start again, somewhere else...

I could have! 'Could have!.. Looking back now...

Tackled him?.. Head-on... Not an easy call, that... 'More harm than good... Let the hare sit... 'Well enough alone...

But it wasn't - nothing well enough about it! And the hare didn't sit!

If only I had!.. Only I had?.. 'Carry that one with me - to the grave...

KNOCK ON DOOR

            (SNAPPING)   Yes-ssss?

ENTER A NERVOUS, UPTIGHT FATHER AIDAN

AIDAN   Father Prior! You won't believe when I...

(BREAKING OFF... PAUSE)

            Are you all right, Father?..

MARK   Do I look all right?

AIDAN   You... Well, to tell the truth, you look a bit washed up.
                     Down! Sorry. Out! Washed out... Sorry.

MARK   Are you jumpy?

AIDAN   No, not at all! No, of course not!

MARK   So will you for God's sake stop fidgeting!

AIDAN   Yes. Yes, of course. Certainly...

MARK   Maybe... maybe you'd be better off sitting down?

AIDAN   No, I'm fine. Honestly. I -

MARK   Sit down!

AIDAN   (SITTING) Yes! Yes, of course! Eh - eh, thank you...

MARK   You can go off people - did you know?

AIDAN   Agreed.

MARK   And some things never change.

AIDAN   Absolutely...

MARK   I'm beginning to think we see eye to eye.

AIDAN   Oh? I - I'm -

MARK   I'll tell you, Aidan. You're my right arm. I don't say you
            are an extension of my right arm - you are my right arm...
            A few more like you and we'd have Merrion Square
            cleaned up in no time.

AIDAN   'Very kind of you to -

MARK   If the Provincial ever thought of transferring you, Aidan,
            I'd fight tooth and nail -

AIDAN   Oh? Oh... I, I wouldn't want you to -

MARK   How's the poetry going?

AIDAN   Oh-hh... Y'know - fits and starts...

MARK   'Ever had a stab at a sonnet?

AIDAN   Well, no... I - I'm more inclined to stay with -

MARK   Ode to a mad monk... To a shanghaied celibate - how
                about that?

AIDAN   Well, I... I mean...

MARK   Six days now, Aidan. Six days. And nights... And still not
                a word -

KNOCK ON DOOR

                (CALLING) Come ahead!

ENTER HUGO.

HUGO   Oh, sorry. I -

MARK   Come in, come in!

HUGO   Well, I -

MARK   You're going to tell me something I won't want to hear?

HUGO   Eh-hh... Yes and no...

MARK   Aidan's about to let me in on something, too - would I be
                right, Aidan?

AIDAN   Well, it's just that - it may be nothing, really -

MARK   Out with it.

AIDAN   A friend of mine, eh - in the Creative Writing Circle -
               she's quite talented, really -

MARK   Right, right -

AIDAN   She eh, she happens to know, know Father Xavier's eh,
               mmm -

MARK   We're with you.

HUGO   No danger of losing us. So far.

AIDAN   And she's told me that the, the lady in question hasn't
               been seen for a few days - left home, abruptly...

MARK   Well, well... Not much poetry in that lot. But thanks all the
               same, Father... Hugo? You're champing at the bit -

HUGO   Ties in with what I have -

MARK   Yes?

HUGO   The Aer Lingus office in Grafton street.

MARK   What about it?

HUGO	Two singles to London bought there on Friday afternoon - cash - for an early flight on Saturday. In the name of -
MARK	Enough! Say no more!..
HUGO	Yes. Yes, I -
AIDAN	However did you come by all that, may I ask?
HUGO	Ah, ah. No names, no pact... Mum's the word.
AIDAN	Oh, dear. Dear, dear. There's a lesson in this for all of us.
MARK	Yes, Aidan.
AIDAN	Well, if you'll excuse me -
MARK	'Course...

AIDAN EXITS.

MARK	Ph-ewwww... 'Means well.
HUGO	Oh, no doubt. It's just - if he wasn't such a wet... That was only a whiff. You should be sitting beside him in the refectory.
MARK	No thanks. I'm bad enough at the top table - the Provincial on one side, Lucifer's lieutenant on the other.

HUGO   Sorry?

MARK   My vicar...

HUGO   Oh... Divil you know, I suppose... Well... at least we have
              a fair idea where he is.

MARK   London. 'Like looking for a needle in a haystack.

HUGO   All we can do is hope and pray... he'll make contact.

MARK   If he's in trouble... No job, funds low.

HUGO   She should be able to get a job. Maybe she was there
              before, for all we know. 'Knows the ropes.

MARK   Ah, it's a mess, no matter what way you look at it.

HUGO   I've a feeling it's going to get worse before it gets better.

MARK   Here, will you have a drink - or will you wait till
              Recreation?

HUGO   I'll have a drink.

MARK   God, that's you all over, Hugo. Straight out...

MARK CROSSES TO A WALL PRESS/CABINET... OPENS IT...
TAKES OUT A BOTTLE AND TWO GLASSES... RUNS A COLD

TAP... POURS WATER INTO A JUG... CROSSES BACK TO THE
DESK... POURS DRINKS... MEANWHILE:

	But at least I know where I am with you... And I have the feeling you wouldn't say anything behind my back that you wouldn't say to my face - not like some of them.
HUGO	You're A One in my book, Mark... Cheers.
MARK	Slainte.... (PAUSE) Father Joe...
HUGO	Hmmm?
MARK	Our man in London. Teaches in some class of a school.
HUGO	Yes?
MARK	Here's one for you: he and Xavier are very close.
HUGO	Oh?
MARK	'Bond between them. 'Goes way back... Sure wasn't it Joe got him into the order in the first place?
HUGO	No, that I didn't -
MARK	Oh, many's the young lad was recruited by Joe over the years he was stationed here.
HUGO	So... so if Joe was here - pastoral work - bringing on

vocations - how come he's now a teacher over in -

MARK   Ah-hh... Sin sceal eile... We're a strange crew, no doubt. We preach charity - supposed to practice it. Some of the time - some of the time - we succeed. And then again, we go and hurt a man - hurt him where it hurts most -

HUGO: His pride.

MARK   'Xavier knows that story, do y'see? 'Knows it well. Would be on Joe's side...

HUGO   So?..

MARK   So Joe's in London. And now Xavier. 'Only a local call away...

Oh, Joe never left the order, still functions as a priest... But because they were friends over the years, Xavier wouldn't be too shy about making contact... And I'll bet you what you like he'll do just that... When he needs help. And he's going to need help - soon now.

HUGO   Money?

MARK   That, yes. Joe's on a salary. Anything he gives Xavier he'll get back from the Provincial account, no problem.

But that's not all... Xavier, y'see, won't get any kind of a half-decent job without a reference... wouldn't be able to open a bank account -

HUGO   So a personal reference from a teacher - ?

MARK   Would be a lot better than a kick in the arse!..

HUGO   Then we wait...

MARK   If he contacts Joe, Joe will ring here... And he'll set up a meeting with Xavier... Some evening, after work... Buy him dinner.

HUGO   And he'll go?..

MARK   'Course he'll go. And to make sure, Joe'll say, no point in posting you a cheque, it'll have to be cash. I'll give it to you when we meet...

HUGO   You're a horrid cute hoor, d'you know that, Prior?

MARK   Do y'think?.. Oh, they'll cry on each other's shoulder over pasta - and a liquid absolution won't go astray...

HUGO   And then?

MARK   Then... Joe'll try his level best to get Xavier to come back - leave the girl...

HUGO   Will he succeed?

MARK   Your guess is as good as mine, a mhic... When a man is in
         his prime - thirty six years of age - tastes the honey for the
         first time, gets to like it's sweetness - it'd be a hard job
         getting him to do a U turn... head back into the desert... to
         sackcloth and ashes...

SCENE 54   GILES IN HIS ROOM.

HE IS DUSTING - HIS DESK, LOCKER, PRESS, BOOK CASE...
LISTENING TO HIS RADIO (WIRELESS OR TRANSITOR?)...

HE CROSSES TO THE RADIATOR, TOUCHES IT...

GILES   Huh!.. And in another hour it'll be stone cold - and won't
          come on again till evening... No consideration... So how
          am I to keep body and soul together?.. And if there's an
          east wind?..

HE CROSSES, PICKS UP A RUG AT THE END OF HIS BED, FOLDS
IT AROUND HIS WAIST AND EASES INTO AN ARMCHAIR... HE
REACHES FOR A NEWSPAPER... THE PHONE ON HIS LOCKER
BEGINS TO RING...

HE MUTTERS, GETS UP, PUTS THE RUG TO ONE SIDE, CROSSES...
SWITCHES OFF THE RADIO, LIFTS THE RECEIVER.

> Yes?.. What?.. Well, get the priest on duty, can't you?..
> How do y'mean, he's not?! He has to be!.. Did you try the
> parlours?.. Well, maybe he's gone round the back to bless
> a new car... What is it, anyway?.. Pregnant?.. Hmmmm...
> Is it obvious?.. Well, then, no need to panic. Let her wait
> around the Mass office... Or put her off till another day...

HE REPLACES THE RECEIVER... TURNS AWAY...

> Huh... Three flights of stairs - down and back - and if the
> lift's not working?..

> For a maternity blessing?.. At my age?..

SCENE 55   THE REFECTORY

A TABLE AT THE END, TO ONE SIDE. (RESERVED FOR THE
BROTHERS.) FOUR OF THE BRETHREN SEATED... TEA...

GEORGE	Sure you wouldn't know what way to look...
JOHN	Ah-hh, here's your brother...
DECLAN	It'll get out all right, nothing surer...
GEORGE	Well, take tomorrow night. Bingo in the hall. More'an

	likely I'd put in an appearance - time it, like, for the interval. And one of them doing the catering - Nellie or Maudy or Trish - would slip me a burger and a cuppa -
JOHN	Fair enough -
SENAN	No harm in that.
GEORGE	But now - now I don't know whether I'll go or not. Afraid I'd - what might be said... or not said...
SENAN	'Dread of a straight question...
JOHN	I know, yeah.
DECLAN	I'm the same meself...
SENAN	Be Gob, we'll all end up confined to barracks!
GEORGE	Under orders - from Xavier!..

SUBDUED LAUGHTER... JOHN INDICATES THE TEA POT.

JOHN	Is there another drop?
SENAN	If it's too strong I can add...
GEORGE	It'll do, rightly...
DECLAN	'Yourself, George?
GEORGE	I'm bad enough without having to get up during the night.
SENAN	I know. Too well I know...
JOHN	Cecil in the Mass Office...
DECLAN	What about him?
JOHN	'Had a woman on to him earlier.
GEORGE	Yes?
JOHN	Very upset -
GEORGE	Oh?
JOHN	A friend - friend of Xavier's... Poor man didn't know what to say... where to look...

SENAN	So he tried the usual - "Not answering his buzzer. If you give me your phone number I'll get him to ring you as soon as..."
JOHN	She wasn't having any! Wouldn't take no for an answer.
DECLAN	Poor Cecil. As a layman, he puts up with a lot...
GEORGE	What could he do?
SENAN	What did he do?
JOHN	'Showed her into Number Two parlour and rang the Prior.
DECLAN	And?
JOHN	'Prior said he was busy, 'get the priest on duty -
GEORGE	Who happened to be..?
JOHN	Father Aidan.
DECLAN	Ah-hh...
SENAN	That's enough!
DECLAN	Oh dear. Dear, dear, dear.
GEORGE	If I'd known what was going on I'd nearly have gone out to her myself.
SENAN	I know, yeah. Sympathy she needed, not scholarship.
JOHN	Cecil says he was in with her for half an hour, give or take. And when she passed the Mass office on the way out she she was using a hankerchief.
DECLAN	Oh, dear, dear...
GEORGE	Did Cecil say what she looked like?
JOHN	Middle aged. No Mona Lisa. But well dressed - smart...
SENAN	Aidan must have told her something.
GEORGE	Enough to let her put two and two together...
DECLAN	So... so what are you trying to tell me? That, that Xavier had more than one female friend here - right here in - ?
SENAN	He's leaving a quare ould trail behind him, no doubt...

DECLAN   So if she knows he's gone away, no one knows where...
              and that this girl, this Emma, is gone away... she, she's
              maybe a bit annoyed?

GEORGE   A bit? I'd say she's hopping mad this minute!

SCENE 56   FINTAN'S ROOM

FINTAN SEATED AT DESK IN HIS ROOM. KNOCK ON DOOR.

FINTAN   Yes?.. Come in...

ENTER AIDAN

AIDAN   Eh, Father... Will you do the needful?..
FINTAN   Of course... Sure...

FINTAN RISES, SEATS HIMSELF IN AN ARM CHAIR ALONG SIDE
THE DESK AS AIDAN CROSSES, KNEELS TO HIM. FINTAN LIFTS
A WASTE PAPER BASKET "OUT OF THE WAY," MAKES THE SIGN
OF THE CROSS...

AIDAN   Bless me, Father, for I have sinned...

SCENE 57   THE KITCHEN

SENAN, GEORGE, JOHN ENTER, CARRYING THE "TEA THINGS"
FROM THE REFECTORY TABLE - MUGS, PLATES, TEA POT, MILK
JUG... THEY CROSS TO THE SINK, RINSE, WASH, DRY, STACK...
MILK TO FRIDGE, TEA POT EMPTIED, TEA BAGS BINNED ETC.

SENAN	Give them here to me...
JOHN	Is there enough milk for morning?
GEORGE	Plenty... What happened to Declan?
JOHN	'Gone up to the Oratory on his way to bed.
GEORGE	Ha. Need I have asked?..
JOHN	He's above there talking to Himself - and we're here -
GEORGE	Yattering...
SENAN	And you may be sure he's saying the prayer for Xavier.
JOHN	If I was as sure of Heaven...
GEORGE	Will we go up to the television room for a while?
SENAN	Ah-hh! What's the use?
JOHN	Even if you get the picture to stop moving, it'll still be all black n white - snow.
SENAN	Smog'd be more like it...
GEORGE	One fag, so, in the Community room and we'll call it a day...
SENAN	So how is the latest change agreeing with ye?..
JOHN	Hmmmm?
SENAN	Us all together at Recreation?
JOHN	Ah-hh... I suppose we'll get used to it after another while.
GEORGE	Maybe it's my age but I preferred it when we were on our

own. The Coffee Room was small, I know, but sure there was never more than the few of us...

SENAN   And all on the same wave length...

JOHN   Now it's hard enough to follow some of them - and you never know what they're going to talk about -

GEORGE   And if you get Father Aidan next to you..?

SENAN   Ah-hh! Good night!..

JOHN   I remember - years ago - Father Emmanuel telling me - the Order at the start was mostly brothers, very few priests...

GEORGE   Change. Change... 'That many changes we won't know after another while whether we're coming or going!

SCENE 58   THE CHOIR/ORATORY

BROTHER DECLAN KNEELING... PRAYING.

Please... Please. You know the score... I don't know the half of it - nor want to... They say he's turned his back on you. I don't believe that. But even if it's true, I know - I'm certain - you won't turn your back on him... Dear Jesus, you haven't got it in you... Oh, please!.. You walked on the waters... Reach out and take his hand. Hold him, don't let him sink... Please, dear Jesus, please!.. Help him... And us...

SCENE 59   THE COMMUNITY ROOM

GEORGE, JOHN, SENAN SEATED... SMOKING...

JOHN	We all have to try and adjust as best we can...
SENAN	Evening Mass, eh?.. There was no evening Mass in my day. Last Mass on a Sunday was the twelve. That was it... And back in the evening, them that had a mind to, for rosary and Benediction. Aye, and a real sermon, likely as not... Not just the few harmless words you get, these times...
GEORGE	Now there's talk o' moving the high altar.
JOHN	And the priest facing the people. What'll it be next?
GEORGE	Well, you have the epistle and the gospel in English now - mark my words, it won't stop there. 'Might even come a day...
JOHN	What?
GEORGE	When - when the whole Mass will be in -
JOHN	Ah, come on!
SENAN	Will you go way outa that, George!
GEORGE	I'm telling you!
SENAN	They'd never go that far!
GEORGE	It's only a matter of time...
JOHN	The consecration?.. God Almighty!..
SENAN	The bread and wine... host... chalice... changed... in, in... English?!
JOHN	Blasphemy, that's what that is - not to put a tooth in it...
GEORGE	In my time every priest said his own Mass - three on a Christmas morning - with an altar boy or a brother serving.

	Now there's talk of con-conceleb-ration.
SENAN	How do y'mean?
GEORGE	One priest says the Mass, the others stand around, waiting their turn to say a bit.
JOHN	Good God!..
GEORGE	I wouldn't mind so much if it was all for the good - but lately, I'm beginning to have my doubts... Let's face it: there's a drop in them coming to Mass, big falling off.
SENAN	I'll go along with that. Us up in the choir looking down: empty seats where before it was standing room only.
JOHN	'Church was always packed on a Saturday night for the novena. Now lookit...
GEORGE	And when the priests go out to hear confessions after, they're back in again by nine and round to the kitchen, looking for their supper.
SENAN	There was a time I never started the fry-ups until coming up to ten -
GEORGE	See what I mean?
JOHN	I'd say television has a lot to do with it.
GEORGE	'Another while, it wouldn't surprise me if we had colour.
JOHN	They say it's on the way right enough -
SENAN	Well, whatever the reason, it's a sad state of affairs, surely, us with a packed hall for Bingo on one side, an empty church on the other -
GEORGE	Even for the first Friday -
JOHN	Or the Holy Hour...
SENAN	It's the people - the people themselves are changing.
GEORGE	Well, do y'see, the respect is gone for the Mass, the reverence that was there in the old days, faded away...

JOHN	I think you're right.
GEORGE	I know I'm right! We've gone all common - common!..
JOHN	John the Twenty Third...
SENAN	What about him?
JOHN	Did he know what he was at, at all at all?..
SENAN	Opening windows, eh...
GEORGE	Letting in... letting out...
SENAN	In the old days you knew where you stood. Black was black, white, white - and a mortlar was a mortlar.
GEORGE	Now it's all greys and question marks and maybes...
SENAN	'Hard to know where you are, most of the time.
JOHN	I'll say that for Father Xavier, he always said Mass with great reverence. 'Put his heart and soul into it.
GEORGE	Whose to say it wasn't just an act?..
JOHN	What!..
GEORGE	Sure he was always acting!.. I'll tell you: if Micheal MacLiammoir was saying Mass up at the Gate they'd be hanging out of the rafters!..
JOHN	Ah, now, that's going a bit far -
SENAN	He - he could be very emotional. 'Took things to heart...
GEORGE	I remember well - not so long ago - coming up to Christmas - or was it soon after?
JOHN	What about it?
GEORGE	When I brought the Sunday papers round here, Xavier was in the door after me. 'Picked up his favourite - The Sunday Times - and I'd swear he went pale.
JOHN	What?
GEORGE	It was across the front page - that priest over in London - leaving to get married.

GEORGE   Davis. Charles Davis.

SENAN   That's him. Caused a few ripples, right enough...

JOHN   Shock waves would be more like it. Terrible scandal. And
            him well got with the Cardinal...

GEORGE   Well, ten minutes later I came back round. The Times was
            gone and so was Xavier.

JOHN   'Took it back to his room to mull over it?..

GEORGE   'Not the first time he fecked it, God forgive me.

THEY STAND, PLACING ARM CHAIRS BACK IN ORDER...

JOHN   What's the latest on him, anyway, I wonder?

GEORGE   Not a whisper. Or if there is, they're keeping it to
            themselves.

JOHN   We'll hear, sooner or later.

GEORGE   Outside, more than likely... Sometimes you hear more
            outside than you do in.

SENAN   George is right. They tell their friends everything, some of
            them...

JOHN   The light's still on in the Prior's office.

GEORGE   There's a few of them in with him, I suppose.

SENAN   Regulars. Three or four in the know.

JOHN   Resolving all the problems of the Universe -

GEORGE   Until tomorrow morning, anyway -

SENAN   And one of the days Mark will hand me the keys of the
            Press and give me the nod - "Supplies running low..."

GEORGE   Time to bin the Dead Men...

SCENE 60   **A CORRIDOR...** SENAN AND GEORGE WALKING.

SENAN	It's weighing on me this past while...
GEORGE	(STOPPING, TURNING) What?
SENAN	I was no help to him...
GEORGE	Xavier?
SENAN	I, I never stopped to think -
GEORGE	What? What, Senan?
SENAN	Well, you know I'm in charge of the press. So I'd give him some on the quiet, now and again. If there was a drop left over from Recreation, maybe a half bottle...
GEORGE	And he'd take it?
SENAN	'Never said no.
GEORGE	'Means he was drinking on his own. Always a bad sign...
SENAN	He was such a good man, in so many ways... 'Helped me a lot when I was, was wavering - if you know what I mean...
GEORGE	Don't be blaming yourself, Brother. You meant well. And anyway, he could have said no. It was up to him...
SENAN	'Kept it in his locker, I suppose.
GEORGE	You can always find somewhere to hide a bottle...
SENAN	Hmmm...
GEORGE	Oh, I knew damn well something was up...
SENAN	How do you mean?
GEORGE	'My room next to his. I'm a light sleeper, not like most of us... 'Heard him getting sick, then running the tap...
SENAN	Oh, dear God...
GEORGE	'Heard him coming in, at night. Oh, late. The early hours, maybe. And not very steady on his feet. He'd come up the back stairs, trying to go easy. 'Tripped a few times...

140

SENAN	Did you not think of saying it to the Prior?
GEORGE	I did but I... didn't... On the tip of me tongue... But somehow, I just couldn't get myself to, to...
SENAN	'Not easy.... to say to one priest about another...
GEORGE	And I didn't know what way he'd take it or what he'd say...
SENAN	Ah, sure, no one likes making a complaint, telling...
GEORGE	You rest easy, Senan. You have nothing to look back on...
SENAN	Ah-hh. Good on you, George... And between ourselves, all right?..
GEORGE	Don't you know?..

SCENE 61   THE PRIOR'S OFFICE

MARK SITS BEHIND HIS DESK, A DRINK TO HAND.
A BOTTLE, A JUG OF WATER, GLASSES ON A SIDE TABLE.
FINTAN, HUGO AND JUSTIN SEATED ACROSS FROM HIM,
DRINKING...

JUSTIN   Oh, I've met brothers who left - sisters - priests who threw
            in the towel. And I ask them, why, why did you?.. It took
            some a while, others didn't hesitate. One way or the other,
            they all came up with the same answer...

HUGO   Which was?

JUSTIN   Lack of humanity...

FINTAN   Hmmm?

JUSTIN   The human touch... Sympathy. Understanding. A warm
            heart...

HUGO   The milk of human kindness, eh? I suppose you're right.

JUSTIN   I know I am!

MARK   Indeed... I've seen it again and again. Promotion from the
            ranks: a curate is appointed a parish priest... a monk
            becomes an abbot... a friar makes it to prior... a sister
            becomes a reverend mother. And overnight - overnight,
            you might say - they cast off the common mantle, assume
            airs and graces...

FINTAN   Present company excluded -

HUGO   Of course!

MARK   I would like to think so.

HUGO   So why, Mark, why do you reckon it happens?

MARK   Power... Authority. "I am someone... I am in charge. I

	make decisions, grant permission - or deny it." And - almost inevitably, this one - "I make changes..."
FINTAN	Ha! A local custom, a house rule, a way of doing things that seemed to work well, was accepted by the community - and along comes the new Boss -
HUGO	Boss being the operative word -
FINTAN	And says - "That'll have to change..."
JUSTIN	It happens. Happens all the time.
HUGO	Stepping on corns. Hurting... And no need for it, nine times out of ten. No need in the wide world.
FINTAN	A new broom.
JUSTIN	One of the lads one day, the next a man of iron...
HUGO	'Not just us. It's everywhere you look.
JUSTIN	Nurses, teachers, the civil service...
HUGO	I have a few contacts in the guards. They tell me things...
FINTAN	Fear. That's what it is - fear of a reprimand, of being overlooked. Fear of a transfer...
HUGO	And no redress, none.
MARK	Not in this world, anyhow...
JUSTIN	So when Xavier got back from Rome, landed on this island of saints and scholars?..
HUGO	I'd say he didn't know what hit him...
FINTAN	We all went through it: one minute you're with twenty, thirty students your own age, all kicking with the same -
HUGO	One day you're polishing the corridor, mopping out the jacks, kneeling for a blessing, asking permission to go outside the gates -
FINTAN	But only if you have another student with you -

HUGO	The next you're home, people calling you father, kneeling for your blessing...
JUSTIN	So Xavier?..
FINTAN	You wouldn't want to know, Justin.
JUSTIN	Hmmm... This I do know: we went through together, were ordained together in the Lateran, side by side. There was never a more single-minded priest...
HUGO	Well... we could all say the same - that first day...
JUSTIN:	So? What happened? Tell me!..
HUGO	He was sent down the country, safe station...
FINTAN	Murdoch... Murdoch was the Prior.
JUSTIN	And?..
HUGO	'Took a turn against him. From the word go. Xavier was hardly in the door, set down his bag.
JUSTIN	But why? If he didn't know him, give him a chance to -
FINTAN	'Hard to believe. Whenever he came to Dublin he was as nice as pie -
HUGO	But when he went back down to his own priory - if everything wasn't to his satisfaction - or even if it was - he let fly. Shouted.
JUSTIN	Shouted?
FINTAN	Yes. Yes, shouted. At Xavier. And he wasn't too particular where...
JUSTIN	How do you mean?
FINTAN	In his room. On the corridor. At the Mass office - people listening...
HUGO	And a few times when Xavier was saying Mass.
JUSTIN	What? Shouted at him? And people in the church!..
FINTAN	From the door of the sacristy. Xavier on the high altar.

144

JUSTIN	'Shaken - to the core. 'Must have been...
HUGO	They say it was about then he got his first bout of asthma.
JUSTIN	'Not surprised... But was nothing said? Done?
FINTAN	A lady - a daily Mass-goer - sat down and wrote a letter. To the Provincial... About Murdoch. Asking - begging... Marked it private, confidential.
JUSTIN	Well, that was something...
FINTAN	I'm told - not sure about this - she never got an acknowledgement...
JUSTIN	Now I've heard everything!
HUGO	I'd love to say you're right...
JUSTIN	What?
HUGO	Nothing was done. That we know of... He had two more years to go before stepping down.
JUSTIN	But the people, the scandal? Did they not -
FINTAN	The people took a lot lying down... It was yes Father, no Father, whatever you say, Father...
JUSTIN	And Xavier? Two more years of THAT?
HUGO	What could he do? Complain? To who? Head office?.. They appointed Murdoch in the first place, he was their man. 'Expect them to turn round and say they had made a mistake?..
JUSTIN	He could have asked for a transfer?
FINTAN	His first year, first assignment?.. How would that look?..
HUGO	Or maybe afraid - 'fraid to open his mouth, draw attention to himself, put pen to paper...
JUSTIN	There it is again... Afraid. Fear...
FINTAN	Nothing in his training would have prepared him...
JUSTIN	Was it then the rot started, I wonder?..

HUGO   You may be sure... 'Started going out. Looking for a
                shoulder to cry on...

FINTAN   Could you blame him?.. There's hardly a man among us
                who hasn't made a friend somewhere along the way...

MARK STANDS, TAKES THE BOTTLE, MOVES FROM ONE TO
THE OTHER, RE-CHARGING... MURMURS OF "THAT'S FINE...
THANK YOU... JUST A DROP..."

MARK   Maybe now ye have a better idea why I was... the way I
                was... with Xavier... Oh, I reckon I know what you're
                thinking: if I had been a bit firmer with him... taken him in
                hand... put it to him that he wasn't playing the game -

HUGO   Something like that, yes.

FINTAN   To be honest...

MARK   'You think that didn't cross my mind? 'Turn it over and
                over in my head?..

HUGO   Then why did you not?..

MARK   Easy enough to turn a blind eye, a deaf ear when a man is
                doing a power of good!.. Outside. And here, in the
                community... I make no bones about it, I liked him. He
                made me smile as he made many a friar smile, betimes...
                And out there, people thought the world of him...

FINTAN   That's on the record.

MARK   And I knew how he fared down the country. Not as much
                as I know now after listening to ye tonight - but enough to
                know he was wounded, in pain. Behind the smile,
                memories - shocking memories...

146

So I went easy on him. At first I didn't notice the sins of omission - or maybe I did but didn't want to, if you follow... Missing out on choir, meditation, 'morning office. Just now and then, at first. But getting more often with the months...

Little things, big things... 'Late for Mass, then rushing it to be off the altar in time for the next... Skipped the sermon, more than once... A downhill slide I should have put a stop to before it got out of hand...

JUSTIN   Mark! Mark, you're gutting yourself... No need.

FINTAN   All you're saying, Prior, is you have a big heart.

MARK   And I made the mistake of thinking with it, not my head!.. Just didn't... see what was ahead.

JUSTIN   Which of us did?..

MARK   'Never thought it would come to...

HUGO   Here's your brother...

MARK   Oh, I thought it would blow over - that he'd go the way of many a man before him in religion: get over it, keep going...

HUGO   'New one on all of us, Prior. New territory...

FINTAN   How were you to know - or any of us?..

MARK   I'll say this for the Pro: 'never gave out to me...

FINTAN   And why should he?!

HUGO   How could he?

JUSTIN   Divil the leg he had to stand on, the same Provincial. 'Never answered a cry of distress from a priory town... left a drunk in charge to run the full term...

MARK   Well, we don't know the ins and outs... There's a lot he has to keep to himself... Any dealings I had with him - 'mightn't be the best communicator in the world - but I'd have to say, I found him a decent enough man...

KNOCK ON DOOR

     Come in!.. Yes?..

GILES ENTERS.

     Ah-hh! Giles!..

GILES   Is there a drop to wet the lips of a poor pilgrim?..

HUGO   Where is he, this stranger?

FINTAN Bring him in, can't you?

MARK   Don't mind them, Giles... Get yourself a glass like a good man...

GILES DOES SO. MARK RISES, POURS...

     I was on my way up to put down the head for the night...

FINTAN Just in time, so. We were thinking of packing it in...

GILES   Thanks, Mark. The blessings of God on you... When what did I see but the light under the door? And the thought came to me, a drop of the creathur wouldn't go amiss this winter night, 'keep the ticker at a steady pace during the long hours of slumber...

HUGO   Be gor, huh! There's a spake...

GILES   (SEATING HIMSELF) What were ye at, anyway?..

148

	Sorting Holy Mother Church?
HUGO	Well... not exactly. There's still one burning issue…
GILES	Oh?..
HUGO	Clerical celibacy.

GILES COUGHS, SPLUTTERS... THE OTHERS SMILE, NOD...

FINTAN	More and more talk about it. Coming from Rome, like.
HUGO	It was Justin filled us in.
JUSTIN	I have it for gospel, not the word of a lie -
GILES	Lookit here to me: I came in for a nightcap - not a poisoned chalice!..

THEY CANNOT KEEP A STRAIGHT FACE... LAUGH OUTRIGHT.

MARK	A bit of order! Let the man have his say...
GILES	Clerical celibacy, huh? A strong tradition - in the Church these hundreds of years... Do away with it? Let priests off the hook? The green light to marry just because they get the hots for some young one?!
FINTAN	Ah, now, Giles! No need to be so crude!
GILES	Crude?! Crude, is it? I'm calling a spade a spade! Damned right, I am!.. And I don't care who said what beyond in Rome – some prick, more'an likely, having trouble with his tay pot.

THEY EXCLAIM IN MOCK HORROR:

JUSTIN	Oh, Giles, Giles! It's worse you're getting!

FINTAN   Come on now, Father - put a brake on it!..

             GILES Married priests? 'Never heard worse... You'd be
             opening the flood gates! What?! In bed at night with a - a
             person of the opposite sex - then vesting the next morning
             to go to the altar, celebrate the sacred mysteries?! Do we
             want to empty the churches altogether?!.. They'd lose their
             respect, the people, turn away in droves... Dear God!
             Squakin' babies... nappies, night feeds... 'broken sleep...
             And that monthly thing that afflicts females... Sure how
             would a man get to say his prayers with all that hanging
             round his neck? I ask you!..

THEY ARE CHOKING AGAIN, TRYING NOT TO LAUGH

MARK   Easy, men, easy...There's people trying to sleep...

HUGO   'One way of looking at it, I suppose – ha, ha!

JUSTIN   Put it like this, Giles. Does it matter - does it really matter
             - whether a priest is married or celibate - as long as he is a
             good... shepherd?

GILES   Huh! Is it one wing I'm to fly on, Prior, this stormy night?

MARK   Oh?!.. Never let it be said, Father... Give us your glass.

GILES   Ah, thank you... 'One for the road.

MARK   'That you can be sure...

GILES   What does it matter, eh?.. Well, I'd say it would matter a
             Helluva lot if the said shepherd was concentrating on just
             the one sheep - and maybe a lamb or two - while the rest
             of the flock was neglected! If you follow...

FINTAN   I'm sorry - with all due respect - that is a non sequitur...

GILES   Oh, do y'hear him! The doctor of canon law, no less!

	It's a wonder, Fintan, you haven't started calling yourself 'doctor' long since - and be done with it!
MARK	Now, now, Giles! No personal remarks! Stick to the mote in your own eye like a good man...
JUSTIN	Look at it this way, Giles. If the Vatican was open to the idea of a married clergy - oh, certain cases, after due deliberation - Xavier might well be still with us...

GILES SLOWLY SETS DOWN HIS DRINK... HE IS SEETHING.

| GILES | Xavier would still be with us if he had said his prayers and done what he was told!.. |

He'd still be with us if he stopped living a lie, a double life...

'Would be still with us if he stopped drinking, stayed in instead of going out, sobered up, put up the pin, maybe, stopped running to confession and started running back to the Lord...

'Stopped making a mockery of the sacrament, making shit of the firm purpose of amendment...

'Made a start to repairing some of the damage - the bad example, horrible scandal - he has given, caused...

I'll say it straight out - and it's not this loosening me tongue, no way! Xavier would be still with us if the likes of ye had looked him in the eye, instead of looking away!

| HUGO | Are you - you trying to say - |
| GILES | 'Not trying to say anything! I'm saying it, straight out, fair and square! Without fear or favour! |

Present company NOT excluded!..

JUSTIN	So... If you were in charge... you would have gone about it - your way. Am I right?
GILES	I won't deny it.
HUGO	Confrontation...
GILES	If you want to use a big word... I call it man to man...
MARK	You'll be telling us next you tackled him?..
GILES	I was waiting me chance. Fuming, I was... A brat, brazen as be damned... Then one morning I was on me own in the refectory when he came gliding in from the kitchen with his coffee, fresh off the altar... I let him have it, I can tell you, no holds barred! He didn't know what hit him!
FINTAN	Did you - did you raise your voice?
GILES	'Raise my voice?!
HUGO	Shout?..
GILES	Did I shout? Did I what! I screamed at the bastard!

THEY EXCLAIM, PROTEST... SHIFTING IN THEIR CHAIRS...

FINTAN	What?!
HUGO	That's going too - !
JUSTIN	Now come on!
MARK	Jesus, Giles!..
GILES	Trying to bring him to his senses, that's all I was doing, get through to him...
JUSTIN	Did he - did he not - ?
GILES	'Sat there staring at me - a rabbit in head lamps...
HUGO	Dear God...
GILES	And nothing putting the brake on me - not like some of the others.

MARK   What?

GILES   He never knocked on my door, knelt to me. 'Never heard
            his confession... But I heard things, rumours in common
            circulation, the brothers coming to me... 'No trouble
            putting two and two together. And no holds barred! 'No
            check on what I said or how I said it...

JUSTIN   So you let fly?

GILES   Damned sure. Told him he was a bloody disgrace – letting
            himself down, the order down!.. Out when he should have
            been in... Cutting corners... The divil riding on his
            shoulder... Drinking... And worse, worse! Womanising...

STUNNED SILENCE

            'Never spoke to me after that. 'Not as much as hello or
            how are you?.. If we met on the stairs or the corridor, he
            looked away, kept going...

HUGO   Would you blame him?

GILES   Too late. 'Got at him too late. The rot had set in... I went
            off on my break soon after, heard the worst when I got
            back...

HE FINISHES HIS DRINK, STANDS, SETS DOWN HIS GLASS.

            And ye can say what ye bloodywell like, I'm not worried!
            I did what I did, said what I said, my conscience is clear!..
            I'll sleep well this night, Fathers, knowing I did my best to
            - to stop a fellow friar doing away with himself... Which is
            a lot more than any of ye can say...

I was told earlier to see to the mote in my own eye. Well, I'm saying the same to ye now - with knobs on!

HE TURNS, STORMS OUT... UNCOMFORTABLE PAUSE.

JUSTIN	Did any of you know - ?..
MARK	No.
HUGO	Not a whisper.
FINTAN	Same here...
JUSTIN	So Xavier... right to the end... one blast after another...
HUGO	'Shell shocked... And keeping it to himself, eh?.. Brooding, hurting... It building up inside him...
JUSTIN	And if he told the girl friend?
HUGO	Ha! More grist to the mill! Fresh ammunition...
FINTAN	Played right into her hands...
JUSTIN	She'd surely use it?
HUGO	If we were as sure of Heaven...

SCENE 62   THE CHOIR   CHURCH BELL TOLLING...

THE BRETHREN STAND, HOLDING BREVIARIES AS THEY RECITE MORNING OFFFICE - LAUDS/THE SMALL HOURS...

AS AT THE BEGINNING (SCENE 2), THIS IS IN MONOTONE, A RATHER RAGGED DELIVERY IN LATIN...

SCENE 63   FATHER PROVINCIAL'S OFFICE

JARLATH SEATED AT HIS DESK... KNOCK ON DOOR.

JARLATH   Come in...

JUSTIN ENTERS HOLDING ENVELOPE.

	Ah-hh... Justin.
JUSTIN	I just got this in the post, Pro.
JARLATH	Oh-hh?
JUSTIN	From Xavier. Just a note. Doesn't say much.
JARLATH	Hmmmm... At least we know he's alive. Now.
JUSTIN	'Knew I was due back... that I'd be staying here for a -
JARLATH	An address? Contact?
JUSTIN	'Phone number. Says if I'm ever in London he'd love to -
JARLATH	Then do. By all means. I'll put something in an envelope for him.
JUSTIN	That would be great. I'll let you know just as soon as -
JARLATH	Oh, and Justin -
JUSTIN	Yes?
JARLATH	Good that the shepherd goes in search of the lost sheep -
JUSTIN	And he is lost, Father Provincial. Reading between the lines, I'm sure of it -
JARLATH	Just don't get carried away. Bring him back if you can - but to this fold? Here?.. No. 'Out of the question. 'Say public Mass? The people would be shocked. The scandal would be even greater than the one already out there...
JUSTIN	Yes.

JARLATH	We - we'd have to work something out. 'Early days yet. So you play it by ear, all right?..
JUSTIN	(TURNING TO GO) 'Will do...
JARLATH	You and he were great friends in the old days?..
JUSTIN	(TURNING BACK) And still are.
JARLATH	Well, then. An old boys' reunion. And Himself presiding?
JUSTIN	Sorry?
JARLATH	Where two or three are gathered together -
JUSTIN	In my name - yes, of course -
JARLATH	Who knows where it might lead?
JUSTIN	(GOING) We live in hope...

EXIT JUSTIN.

JARLATH PAUSES... THEN LIFTS THE RECEIVER, DIALS TWO, THREE DIGITS... WAITS...

JARLATH

Ah, Mark... 'Bit of news, not much... Could you step in a minute?.. And collar the canon lawyer if he's around...

HE REPLACES THE PHONE... PAUSES... PULLS OUT A DRAWER IN HIS DESK, BEGINS TO RUMMAGE...

Now... Where's this I keep the sterling?..

SCENE 64   THE REFECTORY

A SIDE TABLE IN "THE REF". GEORGE SEATED, SIPPING
COFFEE. ENTER HUGO, CARRYING A MUG...

HUGO	Howaya?
GEORGE	I'll do... for another while, anyway...
HUGO	'Here to me: does your man in the kitchen know any other song?!
GOERGE	(SMILING) I'd say he might manage a few lines of the National Anthem at an All-Ireland - like the rest of them...
HUGO	He's in there now with pots and pans, Irish stew and Mary Anne!
GEORGE	Ah, but what a voice! I'm never sure whether he's a bass baritone, a basso profundo - or a brass neck!
HUGO	Did you say voice? He'd come in handy on a ship if the fog horn broke!..
GEORGE	I'll tell him!
HUGO	Would it do any good?
GEORGE	Not a ha'porth!.. Tell us, anyway: what was the traffic like?
HUGO	What?
GEORGE	To the airport. Did you get him away, okay?
HUGO	Just about. Here! How did you know - ?
GEORGE	You were spotted from an upstairs back window going round to the garage. And Justin in his blacks with a hold-all out at the side door...
HUGO	Well, honest to God...

GEORGE	And earlier Brother John brought in the morning post, noticed a London postmark on a letter for Justin... 'knew Xavier's hand from the Mass book in the sacristy...
HUGO	'Getting more like an Agatha Christie every minute...
GEORGE	So how was he? In the car?
HUGO	Ha. Funny you should ask. Quiet. Hardly a word out of him. Not a bit like the Justin we're all used to...
GEORGE	'A lot going through his head. Mulling over what he'll say when they meet up, I suppose...
HUGO	(STANDING UP) Well, I better make a move -
GEORGE	Ah, but wait till I tell you -
HUGO	Don't tell me there's more?!
GEORGE	The Prior was called in -
HUGO	The Pro's office?
GEORGE	And Fintan. 'Best part of an hour now. Whatever's going on...
HUGO	Hmmm. (SARCASM) Well, whatever's going on, George, you'll let me know as soon as you find out, ok?..

SCENE 65   THE PRO'S OFFICE

JARLATH, MARK AND FINTAN IN CONCLAVE...

FINTAN	That's about it. About the best I could manage at short notice.
MARK	You've done well, Fintan -
JARLATH	Indeed... So let me run the last bit past you one more time - just to get it right in my head.
FINTAN	Sure...
JARLATH	Xavier decides he's staying out - wants to make things eh, right - clean the slate - maybe tie the knot?..
MARK	'With you so far...
JARLATH	We draw up a report - put it down on paper - all we know about what was going on...
MARK	Messy enough... God knows.
JARLATH	Then forward the lot to England -
FINTAN	To the diocese where he is domiciled - that's important.
JARLATH	And they take it from there...
FINTAN	They may want to interview him - or they may opt to send the file straight to Rome.
MARK	And then he waits...
JARLATH	No great delay. I understand the present man is making no bones about granting -
MARK	As long as he lasts.
FINTAN	What?
MARK	He's very frail... Justin tells me, seems unhappy.
FINTAN	Xavier's file should cheer him up - Oooops... sorry!
JARLATH	We could all do with a laugh this minute... So the

	document arrives from Rome - secure, sealed. In Latin.
FINTAN	Indeed. Direct to the diocese over there - the Document of Laicisation... Then a priest - someone, say, high up the ladder - contacts Xavier.
MARK	To arrange a meeting?
FINTAN	Ah ha. It'll be up to the cleric, then, to explain what's involved.
JARLATH	Yes?
FINTAN	Once he signs Xavier is reduced to the lay state.
MARK	Reduced?
FINTAN	Reductio ad laicalem - that is the exact term.
MARK	Jesus... All new to me, this.
FINTAN	And without any hope of return - sine spei reddiendi...
JARLATH	Harsh, isn't it?..
FINTAN	It will be explained to him: if he changes his mind at any time in future, wishes to return to the active priesthood -
JARLATH	Yes?
FINTAN	He will not be welcome... And he is strictly forbidden to celebrate Mass or the sacraments coram populo...
MARK;	Coram populo?
FINTAN	Before the people. Publicly.
MARK	Yes?
FINTAN	For fear of giving scandal, I suppose....
MARK	It's them in Rome that are giving scandal. This minute. To me, anyhow... Did you ever come across such coldness?
JARLATH	I suppose they have to cover all loopholes... be precise, clinical...
FINTAN	That's just it. Faceless men in black dealing with a faceless cleric... Just another - statistic.

MARK	But what about an emergency? A sudden accident, say - and no priest for miles?
FINTAN	'Goes without saying... Of course, no question. He could - should - give at least conditional absolution...
MARK	Once a priest, eh-hh... Sacerdos... in aeternum...
JARLATH	So much for the Doomsday scenario... Please God, it will never come to that. Please God....
MARK	We can only hope. And pray.
FINTAN:	Well, if Brother Declan has his way with the Lord, it never will. That man hasn't stopped praying since the news -

KNOCK ON DOOR

JARLATH	Yes?
HUGO	(ENTERING) Just to let you know -
JARLATH	Ah, Hugo! Come in, come in! And shut the door...
HUGO	I got parking near the entrance, went in to make sure he got away.
MARK	So he should be there by now?
HUGO	Just about.
MARK	And now we wait... Justin will make contact just as soon as… What are you thinking... Pro?
JARLATH	Oh-hh... just... Xavier. The first - or the first of many?..

SCENE 66   THE COMMUNITY ROOM

SENAN SEATED IN AN ARM CHAIR, READING A NEWSPAPER...
GILES ENTERS, APPROACHES, SEATS HIMSELF, PICKS UP A
NEWSPAPER...

SENAN	Ah, good day to you, Father.
GILES	Good? Huh! What's good about it?
SENAN	Well, like, as the man says - any day you can get out of bed is a good day...
GILES	(SNIFFING) Is there anything worse than the smell of stale smoke? Wouldn't you think they'd empty the ash trays after them at self?
SENAN	There y'are, that's the way. There's them in this community - and do y'know what I'm going to tell you? - they have as much sensitivity as a bull in hate!..
GILES	Hmmm... I'll have that paper after you - it's me favourite.
SENAN	No bother...
GILES	Good day, how are ya!.. Grey, dismal, damp... Rain clouds down on top of us... You could tip them with your umbrella and you up on the roof...
SENAN	It's pot luck, the climate we have. Whatever muck flies in from the Atlantic and drops on us...
GILES	Hmmm... Why I didn't volunteer for the missions and me still in me prime, I'll never know...
SENAN	'Lot to be said for sunshine and blue skies. And you'd soon get used to the grub. Maize and corn and all like that. A great man, maize, for keeping the bowls regular.

GILES	Right, right.
SENAN	'Can't be bet for roughage. Very few people out foreign, I'm told, have trouble with their behinds.
GILES	If you wouldn't mind... I've had a good breakfast and I -
SENAN	Not like here. I have it for Gospel, every third or fourth one you pass on the street is having problems at the rear... 'Not getting the roughage, do y'see... Porridge is your only man, whatever's in it... Fruit and greens... Aye, and once you hit forty, if you have any sense, you'll let your doctor put on a glove and run his hand up your -
GILES	That's enough out of you, Senan! Will you read the paper for God's sake or give it here to me?!..

SENAN OPENS THE NEWSPAPER AGAIN...THEN STOPS...

	Sure, I mean... something's bound to give... 'stands to reason...
GILES	What?
SENAN	Well, like... if you spend a good part of the day, every day, and you sitting - at a desk, say... or a table... or in an armchair... and you getting on... in your sixties, say, maybe even seventy...
GILES	What about it?
SENAN	Well, God sure!.. Sixty, seventy years... It's a woejus long time to be sitting on the same ould yoke... Do y'know?..
GILES	Look, can you not talk about something else besides your - your nether regions?!

SENAN SHRUGS... RESUMES READING... THEN STOPS...

SENAN	Always a downside - always a -
GILES	Now what?
SENAN	Well, like, you out foreign and the maize kicks in - a sudden, fierce, unstoppable urge to, to divulge yourself -
GILES	Are you off again? -
SENAN	Maybe not a jacks for miles! You frantic! Charging out the back with a spade - only to find the ground rock hard! Aye, and maybe a hoor of a reptile snaking up the back o' your leg ready to sink its poisonous fangs in the, the flab, flabby part of your -
GILES	Shit!
SENAN	Ex-actly! I'm with you there, Father! Let him have it! Oh, absolutely! A dose of his own medicine! No holding back - the full wallop! Bury the fecker! Fumigate the so-n-so! And oh, the relief! Can you imagine? Getting to the top of Everest wouldn't be in it! Then a sturdy bamboo leaf and the job's oxo!..
GILES	Are… you… finished?
SENAN	What?
GILES	The paper…
SENAN	Oh. Oh-hh… Here you are so... I was just checking... 'Nothing...
GILES	(TAKING IT...) What?
SENAN	To see if there was anything - about us. Xavier.
GILES	And d'you think for a minute they'd print it even if they had the story?
SENAN	Well... on the off chance...

GILES	You'd be waiting! Them in Middle Abbey street know better than to run a story showing the Church in a bad light!..
SENAN	John Charles would be down on them, huh?
GILES	Like a ton o' bricks! The Editor of the Indo on the matt in Drumcondra? Ha! That'll be the day...

GILES OPENS OUT THE PAPER, SENAN CHECKS HIS WATCH...

SENAN	So... I better make a move...
GILES	'Here to me a sec: did you ever meet her - this Emma one?
SENAN	No, but I saw her.
GILES	Oh?..
SENAN	Pulling in below, picking him up... That first time, I said to meself - Ah, he's away on a sick call... Maybe an emergency... one of the hospitals, more'an likely... But then it happened again... and again.
GILES	The penny dropped -
SENAN	Then one night I was out late - visiting - and the cousin dropped me home. Pulled in below behind another car and what do y'know, out steps Xavier and makes his way to the side door - none too steady on his feet -
GILES	Oh, dear God. The scandal...
SENAN	And as soon as he's in she's pulling away, driving a bit erratic. Might be a blessing in disguise, says I to meself, if she was stopped by the guards...
GILES	Did the cousin notice?
SENAN	'Didn't come down in the last shower! I passed it over as best I could. But it didn't look right, you know yourself -

him with the habit down to his ankles, her with a skirt maybe above her knees...

GILES   He was playing with fire, small wonder he got burnt... Oh, but there's great rejoicing in Hell this day! The devil and his legions! What?! Bring down a priest, destroy him? Could there be a better reason to be celebrating?.. Satan, Lucifer, Beelzebub and the rest of them..!

SENAN   True for you, Father! Sure God, you could nearly close your eyes and hear the mad laughin' and shriekin' welling up from... from the... the, nether regions...

GILES TURNS HIS HEAD TO STARE AT SENAN

Well... Duty calls... Feed the hungry... And if I don't give them lashings they'll have me guts for garters!..

SENAN EXITS, SINGING:
"Put more turf on the fire, Mary Anne..."

GILES SETTLES AGAIN IN THE ARMCHAIR... MONOLOGUE:

GILES   I wonder does he wash his hands before he starts cooking?.. Don't think about it, Giles. It'd only put you off... 'Head down and hope for the best...

Wouldn't you think the formative years would have knocked some of the corners off him?.. But no... No finesse... None in the wide world... No doubt about it: you can take a man from the bog...

SCENE 67   THE TAILORY

GEORGE BUSY MARKING/CHALKING A LENGTH OF CLOTH
SPREAD BEFORE HIM ON THE WORKTOP...
DECLAN ENTERS, CARRYING A HABIT OVER HIS ARM...

GEORGE	And where might you be going with that?
DECLAN	Orders from on high: the Prior asked me to take it round to you...
GEORGE	His?
DECLAN	Yes. 'Been hanging on the back of his door since -
GEORGE	Say no more. We all remember that day - where we were, what we were at...
DECLAN	Father Mark says you'll know what to do with it...
GEORGE	Xavier's habit - but not his shroud... Well, when it comes back from the cleaners I'll send it down to the noviciate - fit one of the novices, do rightly...
DECLAN	Do y'know, I can still get the smell of smoke off it...
GEORGE	Divil the wonder. He was never able to go long without a fag. Even in Lent...
DECLAN	'Wonder how is he doing now for smokes?
GEORGE	And the price of them over there... 'Could be the silver lining...
DECLAN	How do you mean?
GEORGE	If he hasn't the money?.. No cash, no cigs.
DECLAN	Ah-hh... London'll cure his cough!
GEORGE	And the same with the booze. If he can't afford to drink, he'll have to stop - ease up, anyway...
DECLAN	'Come to his sober senses... 'Always drank coffee in the

morning. Two cups. And the cigarette lit even before the first sip. All he ever had for breakfast.

GEORGE   'Wasn't always like that.

DECLAN   Oh, no! Not at all! One of the best, he was. But lately, like... the last few months...

GEORGE   Since he started seeing your one?..

DECLAN   I suppose, yes... 'Fits...

GEORGE   No doubt, he lost a lot of ground, lately.

DECLAN   Such a nice man, in ways. You wouldn't have the heart to say straight up to him that he was...

GEORGE   Making a dog's dinner of it!

DECLAN   I wouldn't, anyway...

GEORGE   Drink can do a lot of damage if you let it in on you.

DECLAN   I'd say he had a good few getting on that plane.

GEORGE   Out of his mind. 'Had to be...'Should never make a decision when you're drinking - never!..

DECLAN   Our own Father Leo. 'Used to go mad on whiskey. Then one day of a sudden he took the pledge.

GEORGE   Must be twenty years ago, give or take. Hasn't had a drop since, 'that day to this...

DECLAN   New man. Up there in Belfast, right as rain. Working away, well got with both sides...

GEORGE   Killing himself, he was. He'd be dead now, only he put up the pin. Oh, long since. Nothing surer...

DECLAN   So if Xavier was to go in somewhere? For a cure, like?

GEORGE   It'd have to be a complete overhaul. Take him apart, put him together again... 'Take weeks, maybe...Would he be up to it, I wonder?..

DECLAN   With God all things are possible...

GEORGE	He'd have to come out again very - single-minded. I'll tell you, Brother Declan: he'd have to want Jesus Christ the way a drowning man wants air...
DECLAN	'Should be the way with all of us, I suppose...

JOHN ENTERS.

GEORGE	Ah-hh... The hard...
JOHN	It's a while now since I was up a ladder.
DECLAN	What?
JOHN	The Prior wants me to paint the empty room on the second floor. I'm to take my time, do a thorough job. Walls, ceiling, door, window...
GEORGE	You don't sound too happy, John?..
JOHN	Oh, I'll manage. 'Have the transistor on while I'm at it... 'Distract me.
DECLAN	What?
JOHN	From thinking too much about the friar who once -
DECLAN	You'll be painting with a heavy heart?
JOHN	Easy enough to paint a room... refresh it... bring it back up to what it was... 'Not so easy to... to -
GEORGE	'Stop thinking about the man who had it not so long ago.
JOHN	And when I finish, pick up my tattle - bits and pieces - step out into the corridor...
DECLAN	Pull the door after you...
JOHN	The smoke will be gone - and the smoker... For all the fresh paint and smell of turps, it'll still be an empty room...

SCENE 68   THE KITCHEN

SENAN BUSY. HE TURNS FROM THE COOKER TO THE WORK
UNIT, HOLDING A LARGE SAUCEPAN. HE USES TWO FORKS TO
LIFT A QUANTITY OF SPAGHETTI AND HOLD IT ALOFT FOR A
MOMENT OR TWO TO DRAIN...
EVEN AS HE DOES SO HE IS SINGING:

"Oh-oh, Mary my dear, be of good cheer...
And shlap down an ould sod on the fire..."

CHURCH BELL RINGING... AND FADE...

SCENE 68   THE CHOIR

THE BRETHREN: SOME KNEEL... SOME SIT SILENTLY... ONE
CHECKS HIS WATCH... ANOTHER STIFLES A YAWN...

KNOCKING: KNUCKLES ON WOOD...

ALL RISE... A CANTOR SINGS:

Tota pulchra es, Maria...

ALL JOIN IN...

A BRIEF HYMN BUT VERY LOVELY WHEN SUNG WELL,
UNACCOMPANIED...

Tota pulchra es, Maria...

Et macula originalis, non est in te.

Et macula originalis, non est in te...   etc.

TO THE FINAL LINE:

Virgo Maria...

SCENE 69   A SEQUENCE OF "QUICKIES..."

THE TAILORY

GEORGE LOOKS UP AS DECLAN HURRIES IN:

DECLAN   He's back!.. In the front door this minute!..

THE KITCHEN

SENAN TURNS FROM THE COOKER AS JOHN HURRIES IN:

JOHN   Back! Justin! Gone straight up in the lift!

THE REFECTORY

GILES AT COFFEE BREAK AS SENAN BURSTS IN:

SENAN   Back! Justin! 'This minute!..

FINTAN'S ROOM.

HE LOOKS UP FROM HIS DESK AS HUGO ENTERS:

HUGO   On your marks! Get set! Justin's back!

SCENE 70   THE PROVINCIAL'S OFFICE

 JARLATH RESPONDS TO A KNOCK ON HIS DOOR:

JARLATH   Yes?..

MARK ENTERS.

MARK   He's back...
JARLATH   And?..
MARK   Tight lipped. Gone up to his room to change...

JARLATH   Father Fintan?..

MARK   I have him on stand-by.

JARLATH   Do, then...

MARK CROSSES TO THE HOUSE PHONE ON THE PRO'S DESK,
LIFTS THE RECEIVER, DIALS TWO, THREE DIGITS... PAUSE.

MARK   Fintan?.. The Pro's office... Now...

RECEIVER CRADLED

If it's a negative..?

JARLATH   I don't want to think about that... until I have to...

KNOCK ON DOOR

Come in...

JUSTIN ENTERS... TUGGING AT HIS HABIT, FIXING HIS COWL...

Ah, Justin...

MARK   Have a seat, Father... Relax, take your time. We're not
going anywhere...

THE DOOR AGAIN OPENS AND FINTAN ENTERS.

JARLATH   Come in, Father. Shut the door.

FINTAN DOES SO BUT STAYS "ON THE FRINGE OF THINGS..."

JUSTIN	(NODDING TOWARDS FINTAN) Fintan...
FINTAN	You're welcome back, Justin.
JUSTIN	Thanks... So look. To put it bluntly, no. And that's how it stands. No...
JARLATH	Hmmm... A definite no?
JUSTIN	I wouldn't say that...
MARK	How do you mean?
JUSTIN	The man's in bits. It took a lot out of him to do what he - what he did.
JARLATH	Only to be expected, I suppose...
JUSTIN	'Didn't know where to look when we met. 'Walked into a wall, nearly, he was so embarrassed... I gave him the envelope. He was very grateful - said to thank you.
JARLATH	'Help with the rent, put a coat on his back for the winter...
MARK	Has he a job?
JUSTIN	Mickey Mouse... Six days a week. Half day on Saturday. 'Has to clock in every morning, nine on the button.
MARK	Clock in? Xavier?!! Clock?! I don't believe it!..
JUSTIN	'Dead serious. I'd know if he was joking...
MARK	Good God! What he left - what he went to!..
JARLATH	Wages?
JUSTIN	Buttons...
MARK	Bread on the table - but no butter?
JUSTIN	Something like that...
JARLATH	So... Is there someone?..
JUSTIN	Yes.
JARLATH	Did you meet her?
JUSTIN	Briefly.
MARK	How did you find her?

174

JUSTIN	'Looked me in the eye. 'Didn't blink.
MARK	Stared you down?..
JUSTIN	You could say that, yes...
MARK	Unflinching, you might say?
JUSTIN	Correct.
MARK	(TO JARLATH) She has him...
JARLATH	Has she a job?
JUSTIN	'Of sorts. 'Nothing much - as far as I could -
MARK	Huh! Minnie Mouse!..
FINTAN:	(CHOKING BACK A LAUGH) Sorry... Sorry, I -
JUSTIN	Mouse? No way. Anything but!
MARK	You don't seem to be mad about her?..
JUSTIN	I - I'm sure she has her points... She, she knows what she wants.
JARLATH	Does he know what he wants?
JUSTIN	'Not black and white - no.
JARLATH	Did you put it to him, that he could still - ?
JUSTIN	Indeed. Man to man... A retreat in the Cenacle - for as long as it takes... Then fly him out. A diocese in the States. Square the bishop. Or not?.. Maybe what he doesn't know?.. 'Might be glad of a priest from Ireland... 'Knows English and all...
JARLATH	And?..
JUSTIN	He just shook his head. Not as easy as that. Y'see...
MARK	What?
JUSTIN	They - they're sleeping together...
MARK	So?.. What's new?
JUSTIN	She may be...
MARK	What!? But sure contraceptives are on sale over there -

openly! He could buy a packet across the counter!

JUSTIN   Out of the question. As far as I could -

JARLATH   An added complication. But even if she is - pregnant. There's still a way back.

MARK   Adoption.

JARLATH   Good living Catholic family. 'Glad of a baby. 'Bring it up well...

MARK   Wouldn't be the first time...

JARLATH   Free him up. To do a retreat. Prayer. Counselling...

JUSTIN   All he knows is...

MARK   Yes?

JUSTIN   She wouldn't hear of it. He, he mentioned it to her once - eh, the possibility.

MARK   And?..

JUSTIN   She went through the roof!

MARK   Huh. 'As old as the hills, that one.

JUSTIN   Handcuffs...

JARLATH   So he'll be torn - pulled one way, dragged another.

MARK   Stand by his child - or bail out.

FINTAN   'Leaving mother and child to... manage?

JARLATH   Hmmm... Stalemate.

JUSTIN   'Knowing him as I do...

JARLATH   What?

JUSTIN   He wouldn't be able to turn his back on, on -

FINTAN   His own... flesh and blood.

MARK   We could offer to support her - for a while, anyway.

JARLATH   No. No question...

JUSTIN   I - I offered him absolution as we were -

MARK   Yes?

JUSTIN	'A great sadness in his eyes. He said - Would it work?..
FINTAN	Well... he's living with her. Where would that leave his firm purpose of amendment?..
JARLATH	To make a long story short, Justin: you found him in bits, you left him in bits?..
JUSTIN	That's about it... Sorry it's not more -
JARLATH	You have our gratitude, Father. No one could have done - 'Up to us now. 'Over a month since Xavier... Well, then... We can put it off no longer. Canon Law... Fintan, what does it say again in the Ritual? The exact wording...

FINTAN OPENS A BOOK... READS:

	Eh-hh... "Having taken flight with a female... and showing no signs of remorse or contrition..."
JARLATH	And the line after that..?
FINTAN	"The calendar month since his departure from the cloister without permission having now expired..."
JARLATH	See. We have no choice... Tomorrow, then. In the refectory. Before the dinner. Say about ten to one... Shouldn't take long.
MARK	I hate the thought.
JARLATH	How do you think I feel?
MARK	I'll board a notice... Give recreation tonight, break it to them then.
FINTAN	Xavier need never know...

SCENE 71   THE REFECTORY

THE REFECTORY. A SIDE TABLE... AIDAN SEATED, READING.
JUSTIN ENTERS, HOLDING A COFFEE MUG...

JUSTIN	Ah-hh... Aidan. Father Aidan. 'Haven't seen much of you since I got here...
JUSTIN	Ah, sure, I'm out at the school most days... I'm sure I was the last to hear about Xavier...
JUSTIN	Did you hear I was over to London to meet him?
AIDAN	We all have that... How did you find him?
JUSTIN	More than a bit lost. Very unsure of himself.
AIDAN	'Doesn't sound a bit like him...
JUSTIN	'Different ball game now. He's in a different league...
AIDAN	You and he were great friends over the years?..
JUSTIN	The best...
AIDAN	Wasn't an easy call so?..
JUSTIN	Anything but...
AIDAN	To be honest, he was not a great favourite of mine...
JUSTIN	Oh?
AIDAN	His bouncing around - hail fellow, well met - all things to all men - a smile and a joke for everyone that came his way - frankly, it left me cold. I never quite knew what to make of him...
JUSTIN	Well, I -
AIDAN	I was an easy target for his jokes... his teasing... He could be cruel - especially when he had drink taken...
JUSTIN	For all that, he had a way with the people that you might have...

AIDAN	Resented?..
JUSTIN	Something like that.
AIDAN	'Could well be... I suppose in a way I was jealous - he had gifts and talents that were beyond me...
JUSTIN	Well, if you were to see him today...
AIDAN	I can only imagine...
JUSTIN	'One of the times we met. I knew there was something gnawing at him - 'took the wind out of my sails when he told me.
AIDAN	Yes?
JUSTIN	He was hearing confessions out there in the church one evening. A man came in to him - away from Mass and the sacraments for longer than he could remember - he was to be best man at a wedding the next day... Xavier lit on that. "Only going because..." He had been drinking, Xavier - or was hung over, 'can't remember which... This he does recall, vividly - a memory he'll take with him to the grave: he ate that man, dressed him down, scolded him...
AIDAN	Oh. Oh, dear God... They - they say if you are bullied, you will bully, in turn...
JUSTIN	The man walked... out of the confessional... out of the church...
AIDAN	Never to return, for all we know...
JUSTIN	Xavier - the pain in his eyes, on his face - "If I could meet that man again - I know it's impossible, out of the question - but if I could, if I came across him again - somehow, by some chance - I would go on my knees to him, kiss his feet, beg his forgiveness..."

SCENE 72   THE COMMUNITY ROOM.

THE BRETHREN AT RECREATION. ALL EXCEPT JARLATH.
WELL UNDER WAY. FOCUS ON ONE GROUP, THEN ANOTHER...

GROUP A

OFF CENTRE: MARK, JUSTIN, DECLAN SEATED, DRINKING...

MARK	Okay, it will be okay, Declan... 'Not to worry...
DECLAN	But - but the High Altar?! Move? How can it be - ?!
MARK	Look, Brother... Oh, your turn, Justin - I'm getting hoarse!
JUSTIN	'No sweat, Declan. The High Altar won't be touched - just made obsolete.
DECLAN	Obsolete?! The Hi-High Altar?
JUSTIN	No. No, look. It will be left standing, as is. But it won't be used any more.
DECLAN	But, but -
JUSTIN	A smaller altar will be put up in front of it - nearer the people -
MARK	And that's where the priests will say Mass from then on -
JUSTIN	The smaller altar will look more like a table - the table of the Lord -
MARK	And the priest will face the people - they'll see what he's doing, hear what he's -
JUSTIN	Taking all the old mystery out of it - no more standing with his back to them, them not knowing what he's at -
MARK	You'll see, Declan. It'll all settle into place in jig time -
JUSTIN	The people won't know themselves after another while -
DECLAN	Oh, I don't know...

180

JUSTIN	And once the communion rails are removed -
DECLAN	The communion rails?!
MARK	There'll be less of a barrier be-between celebrant and congregation.
DECLAN	But the people - where they knelt and closed their eyes, put out their tongues -
JUSTIN	No. No, the emphasis will be on standing, walking up to receive -
DECLAN	And the altar rails? What will happen to - ?
MARK	We'll jump that one when we come to it. 'Early days yet. We'll have to have a think about it.
DECLAN	Jesus, Mary and Joseph! Where are we going at all, at all?!
MARK	Going back to the early days of the Church, that's where we're going, Declan.
JUSTIN	Back to when it was a simple meal - the breaking of bread...
MARK	When a loaf - once broken up - could feed a multitude...

GROUP C

AIDAN, HUGO AND GEORGE SEATED IN A SEMI-CIRCLE.

GEORGE	Fair play to you, Father Hugo, your few words on Sunday at the twelve - spot on!
HUGO	Ah, thanks, George. Kind of you to -
GEORGE	And no plamas, Father. I wouldn't say it if I didn't -
HUGO	Sure I know that, George. Only too well I -
AIDAN	Those down the back or in the porch couldn't but take it in...

GEORGE	You were there?
AIDAN	In the choir...
HUGO	Oh-hh... Well, I'll tell you: if I was to hammer that home - Domine, non sum dignus - every single Sunday for a year, I'd consider it time well spent!..
AIDAN	And how right you'd be -
GEORGE	How's this you put it, Father?
HUGO	No man, no angel, is worthy to receive. We do so, not because we are worthy - but despite the fact that we are -
GEORGE	That's it! That's the phrase - despite!
HUGO	Unworthy...
GEORGE	Well, more power to you, Father... 'Just thinking, if only Xavier had been above in the choir - or in the sacristy - to hear -
HUGO	Are you joking, George? Sure it was from Xavier I first heard it put like that and us out giving a mission!
GEORGE	Ah, go way!.. And was he listening to what he was saying, I wonder?
AIDAN	Practising what he preached...

TABLE B

GILES, FINTAN, JOHN, SENAN... DRINKING... LAUGHING...

FINTAN	A few pints in his local after the twelve Mass...
GILES	The divil mend him!
FINTAN	'Leaves the pub and wanders off on his own... Through a

woods, comes to a river... 'Crowd o' people standing, up to their waists... This man ducking them, one at a time -

SENAN   That'd be baptising, I suppose -

JOHN   Total immersion -

GILES   Hush, will ye, hush?! Let him tell the joke -

FINTAN   So the drunk jumps in and wades over. The head man frowns when he gets the smell of drink, says - "Have you found Jesus?" The drunk shakes his head - No. So your man gets him by the shoulders and dunks him! Brings him up again... Spluttering, coughing, gasping... "Have you found Jesus?!" No!
            'Gets him by the shoulders and dunks him again - This time he holds him down a bit longer. Brings him up. More gasping for air, choking.
            "Have you found Jesus?!" The poor fella at his wits' end: "No!.. Are - are you sure this is where he fell in?.."

LAUGHTER... AD-LIBBING...

GILES   I might be able to use that one in one of my sermons - I'm down for a mission in Lent.

AT TABLE C   HUGO CHIMES IN - CALLS ACROSS:

HUGO   You could do worse, Giles!

GILES   What's that supposed to mean?!.

HUGO   Put it into your sermon on charity - fraternal forgiveness...

GILES   Just you watch your own slate!

THE PRIOR STANDS TO ADDRESS THEM:

MARK   If I can have your attention, please... What I have to say
        now is straight from the Provincial's office... He asks all
        members of the community that are free to join him
        tomorrow in the refectory just before dinner... at ten to
        one, to be exact...

        Yes, you've probably guessed - to do with Xavier... He has
        to tie a few loose ends, knot a few strings... 'There in black
        and white in the Code of Canon Law... 'Has no choice but
        to... So...

        I'll leave ye and love ye.

        May we all find Jesus this night... And every day and night
        along the way ahead.

EXIT MARK. THE BRETHREN SIT IN SUBDUED MOOD...

DECLAN   Lo-loose ends... Knot a few... What does he mean, Father
         Justin?
JUSTIN   Well, Declan... God love you... Over there in Rome, they
         want everything to be neat, ordered... They're saying
         Xavier is either in or out, one way or the other. He's gone
         now, well over the month as it is –

GILES	Why don't you tell it as it is, Justin? Straight up?! 'A spade a spade!.. Your precious Xavier, Declan, tomorrow at ten to one, is to be officially declared excommunicated!
DECLAN	Oh... Oh-hh...
GILES	Aye, and rightly so!

DECLAN RISES, DISTRAUGHT... EXITS... JOHN STANDS UP.

JOHN	I - I'll go after him...
FINTAN	You'd only be interrupting, John. He's already talking to the Lord this minute...
JOHN	Oh-hh... I suppose...
HUGO	That spade you're talking about, Giles - would you ever go out to the garden, dig a hole and bury yourself in it?!
GEORGE	Ho! Ho! The knives are out!
GILES	I'm not here to be made a laughing stock of!
HUGO	No, you're here to throw oil on troubled waters!.. Sure who could be blamed for confusing you with the Good Samaritan?!
GILES	You've no respect for your elders, that's your trouble, Hugo! For them that bore the heat of the day and the trials and troubles thereof!
JUSTIN	Come on now, men, order, a little order! –
SENAN	I'll have a baby cham!..

LAUGHTER... THE TENSION IS SUDDENLY DISPELLED...

GEORGE	More power to you, Senan!
JOHN	You never lost it, Brother!

SENAN   Never had it to lose!

AS THE BONHOMIE SUBSIDES:

AIDAN   I've come across it in G K Chesterton...

GEORGE   What?

AIDAN   His theory about God - a God forever laughing at us but
             his laughter is so, so high- pitched we cannot hear it...

GEORGE   Oh, yes?..

AIDAN   Set me thinking about Xavier. Maybe - just maybe - he
             was calling out for help - shouting - oh, screaming! - and
             his call was so high pitched, we didn't hear it...

HUGO   Or simpler, still - all the signs were there but no one was
             bothering to read them..?

AIDAN   Because we were taken up with trivia, preoccupied with
             minutiae?..

GEORGE   You've lost me, Fathers. A bit, anyway...

HUGO   (LAUGHING) Here's your brother, George!..

GEORGE   Look, what I don't understand - may never understand this
             side of the grave - is why he didn't turn to someone, ask
             for...? Why he didn't have the guts, the gumption, to turn
             to... them in charge, the ones over him... and put his cards
             on the table - like a man!.. Instead of slinking off into the
             night like a, like a spineless scavenger!..

HUGO   There's a spake and a half!

AIDAN   Delivered with Ulster gusto!

JOHN   I'm with George on that!.. Why didn't he?.. The brothers,
             like - among ourselves - have tried to work that one out -

SENAN   And always came up against a brick wall -

JOHN	Why? Why didn't he?!.. The Prior, his local superior... The Provincial, himself - just down the corridor, he only had to knock!.. After all, he's supposed to be the servant of us all!
JUSTIN	If only it was as black and white as that, John -
JOHN	So why isn't it?!
GEORGE	We're a family, right? One of the sons of that family has a problem - his conscience maybe, giving him Hell - so how come he doesn't go to the father of the family -
SENAN	For help, guidance, advice -
JOHN	Love…
GILES	(INTERJECTING) Remember man, thy last end and thou shalt never sin. Simple as that…
HUGO	'Nothing simple about it - and no easy solution...
JUSTIN	You're very quiet there, Fintan?..
FINTAN	'Just thinking... Five weeks ago we were running here, rushing there, phoning around - searching for Xavier... Now - here - tonight - we've started searching… our hearts...
HUGO	And what are we finding? Each one with a different take on Xavier. Not one of us that hasn't his own memories.
GILES	He who puts his hand to the plough and looks back -
FINTAN	Each with his own measure of guilt... Turning the blind eye, the deaf ear...
HUGO	Sins of omission...
GILES	Is not fit for the Kingdom of Heaven...
FINTAN	Did he run away or did he... vote with his feet?

MURMURING... UNEASE... SHIFTING...

SENAN   What?

FINTAN   If he was given a raw deal over the years -

one knock after another -

Bullied, shouted down, screamed at, lied to -

A pawn in a game of inhouse politics -

Left in Limbo under a lunatic prior, crazed with alcohol...

Look! See what I'm saying! Okay, I exaggerate -

to make my point - but not that much...

They gave him a kick in the goolies, the powers that be.

Was he to turn to them, then - smile sweetly:

"Ah, Fathers. You've treated me like shit - no matter that.

Right now I'm in need of some spiritual direction..."

Well, men... How about that for a scenario?

Nearer the mark, would you say? Closer to the bone?..

HUGO   'Uncomfortably so...

GILES   Rubbish! Never heard such a - !

GEORGE   Another way of looking at it, no doubt...

SENAN, JOHN NOD... ASSENT...

FINTAN   There's them will say he lost his vocation -

GILES   Lost? Lost! He threw it away - flushed it down the jacks!

FINTAN   'Them who'll say he lost his faith... Or would it be nearer

home to say?..

SENAN   Hmmm?

FINTAN   He lost his belief... in...

JOHN   What?..

188

FINTAN   Us…

PAUSE… GILES SETS DOWN HIS GLASS, STANDS UP…
STORMS OUT ON:

GILES   If it was the army he'd be a deserter… caught…
              court-martialled… stood against a wall and…

DOOR SLAMMED SHUT… PAUSE

HUGO   Are you - let me put it like this - are you saying he'd rather
              be in London, rubbing shoulders with all sorts, than here -
              with us?

FINTAN   Something like that…

JUSTIN   His last night… in his room… under this…

GEORGE   What?

JUSTIN   Will I? Won't I?.. A rare torture…

FINTAN   Kicked when he was down - again and again - and no one
              thought for a minute that he would - retaliate -

HUGO   Not the way he did - not to such an extreme -

FINTAN   Least of all, the powers that be. Their turn for a blast of
              Arctic air, a reciprocal kick in the goolies!..

JOHN   There's an eye-opener for you…

AIDAN   At the end of the last Chapter, I met Xavier on the first
              landing, holding a letter from the Provincial's office. Two
              lines telling him he was out of a job... "It has been decided
              that..." I felt sorry for him, he was - winded.

JUSTIN   But surely it was explained to him..?

FINTAN   No.

JUSTIN	No one take him aside, a word in his ear?..
FINTAN	Not that I ever heard...
GEORGE	There's brotherhood for you!
JOHN	Family how are you!..
JUSTIN	A few weeks from now, I'm back in Africa... 'have a feeling, I'll never see him again...

PAUSE... UNCOMFORTABLE SILENCE

SENAN	Here! Here now! Is it Recreation we're at or what? Is this the community room - or an undertaker's parlour? I'll tell you, I've had more fun at a wake!..
JOHN	Come on now, Senan! It's not exactly time for a jig and a reel!
SENAN	I know! But this would get anyone down!
GEORGE	He's right, y'know. Senan's right. 'Mustn't let it get to us.
JOHN	Give in -
SENAN	That's more like it! Now you're talking!.. 'Tell you what: if we get round Justin he'll surely give us a few bars!?

ASSENT... RISING ENTHUSIASM...

JUSTIN	Ah, no. God, no...
FINTAN	Do, Justin, do! As only you can sing it - Mary Anne!
JUSTIN	Ah-hh... I don't -
JOHN	Cheer us all up!
GEORGE	Pull us out of the depths...
HUGO	Come on, Justin! Give us a blast!
FINTAN	'Way you used sing it when we were students in Rome –

HUGO	'Many's the summer's night under the orange trees...
JUSTIN	Well... just a verse...
JOHN	Good on you, Father! Good man -
SENAN	Ciunas, now, please! Could we have a bit of ciunas for the singer?!

JUSTIN	"Oh, my name it is Patsy Maloney... from the hilltops near Mullinahone,
	I'm in love with a sweet little coleen and I hope soon to make her my own...
	She lives with her father and mother in a sweet little cot by the mill.
	And wherever in life I may wander sure I'll think of that darlin' spot still..."

SENAN	All together now, lads -

ALL	"Put more turf on the fire, Mary Anne, for the weather is dreary and cold,
	Shlap down an ould sod, Mary Anne, for we're both growing feeble and old...
	And we'll talk of ould times, Mary Anne, and the troubles of life we've been through
	that has turned this ould world nearly upside down but never changed my love for you..."

SENAN	Second verse if you please!..

JUSTIN ATTEMPTING TO SING, BREAKING DOWN...

"Ah Mary and do you remember...
that night... down... the little... boreen... "

HE STOPS... UNABLE TO CONTINUE... FUMBLING A
HANKERCHIEF TO HIS EYES...

HUGO STANDS, BEGINS TO SING WHERE JUSTIN LEFT OFF...
HE CROSSES, PLACES A HAND ON JUSTIN'S SHOULDER...

"When I whispered the fond loving words, dear, down by
the purling stream...
And we watched the ould smoke curlin' up from your ould
fella's cabin close by
Ah, now Mary my dear be of good cheer and slap down
that ould sod on the fire."

SENAN   Gusto, now, lads! Give it a lash!   (CHORUS)

HUGO   "Now let us be pleased and contented and pass down my
good ould dudeen
And we'll drink to your love and mine, dear, with a wee
little drop of poteen,
And we'll talk of good days in old Ireland, the days that
we all do desire...
Ah, now, Mary my dear be of good cheer and put down
an ould sod on the fire..."

SENAN   Now! Your besth! Your almighty besth!

ALL   "Put more turf on the fire, Mary Anne, for the weather is dreary and cold,

Shlap down an ould sod, Mary Anne, for we're both growing feeble and old...

And we'll talk of ould times, Mary Anne, and the troubles of life we've been through

that has turned this ould world nearly upside down but never changed my love for you..."

UNTO CRESCENDO.

"But never changed my love for you... Mary Anne..."

MORIENDO

"but never changed my love for you..."

THE END

ADDENDUM

MARY ANNE

Moderato

OH MY NAME IT IS PAT-SY MA- LON — EY FROM THE
HILL TOP NEAR MULL-IN-A- HONE _____ I'M IN
LOVE WITH A SWEET LIT-TLE COL ___ LEEN AND I
HOPE SOON TO MAKE HER MY OWN _____ SHE
LIVES WITH HER FA- THER AND MO ___ THER IN A
SWEET LIT- TLE COT BY THE MILL _____ AND WHERE-
-EV-ER IN LIFE I MAY WAN ___ DER- SURE I'LL
CHORUS
THINK OF THAT DAR-LIN' SPOT STILL _____ PUT MORE
TURF ON THE FIRE MA-RY ANNE _____ FOR THE
WEA-THER IS DREA-RY AND COLD _____ SHLAP

DOWN AN OUL' SOD MA—RY ANNE ———— FOR WE'RE
BOTH GROW—IN' FEE—BLE AND OLD ———— AND WE'LL
TALK OF OLD TIMES MA—RY ANNE ———— AND THE
TROU—BLES OF LIFE WE'VE BEEN THROUGH ———— THAT HAS
TURN'D THIS WHOLE WORLD NEAR—LY UP — SIDE — DOWN BUT
NEV—ER CHANGED MY LOVE FOR YOU (AH NOW ——)
YOU ———— MA—RY ANNE ———— BUT
NEV—ER CHANGED MY LOVE FOR YOU ————

(WORDS OF VERSES 2 & 3 OVER)

Circa 1982. Drama studio, Radio Centre, RTE, Dublin 4.
(Credit: Jonathan Ryan.)

Writer; Producer/Director; former Head of Drama, Radio, RTE.

His scripts have been broadcast on RTE, Radio One,
BBC 4 and, in translation, on European networks;
televised on RTE One, BBC One and Channel 4;
staged at the Peacock by the Abbey National Theatre,
at the Project, the Liverpool Playhouse
and on the London Fringe…

Has lived and worked in communications all his life:
subeditor, editor, journalist, producer, director, writer…
Radio has been - always will be - his first love.
"Radio makes the best pictures…"
'Fell in love with Hiberno-English a long time ago
and has been in love with it ever since…

Credits include

The Night of the Rouser.   Earwig.

The Dreamers.   Fugitive.   Veil.

Penny for Your Travels.   Far Side of the Moon.

Three for Calvary.   Pilate Under Pressure.

Jenny One, Two, Three…

The Circus.   Centre Circle.   Gluepot.

Where Do We Go from Here, My Lovely?

At The Praetorium.   Conclave.

Assault on a Citadel.

Also on Amazon: *Notes on the Past Imperfect. At the Praetorium.*
Veil. Pilate Under Pressure. Good Friday Revisited. Etc.

Has facilitated many workshops on Creative/Script Writing
in Dublin and at various centres around Ireland.

www.sean-walsh.me

January 1991. Siobhan's birthday card to her Dad, the last par:

*"I hope that you put on paper all that has happened in your life, even though it
would probably hurt you, and then probably your soul would begin to heal, and
the rest of the world would have a great play to see!!"*

Forget the public. *"The farther away from the public a book is written the
more powerful it is."* - Pere Gratry. *Les Sources.*

*"The best work that anybody ever writes is the work that is on the verge of
embarrassing him, always."* - Arthur Millar.

"Writing? Easy. You just sit down at a typewriter - and bleed…"
                    - Ernest Hemingway.

"There is no greater agony than bearing an untold story inside you."
                    Maya Angelou.

Sean Walsh

Notes On The Past Imperfect

Amazon.com Amazon.co.uk et al Paperback.

May, '14. A letter I received in the post... I share a taste of it - but not the name and address of the writer. I shall cherish it for always...

"Dear Sean,

Your book, Notes on the Past Imperfect, spoke right to my heart. I cried a lot reading it but also smiled at parts... It touched me to the core of my being... You have a deep understanding of matters of the heart... Thank you for your truth and honesty written in these precious pages... You have helped me on my own journey... Just want you to know how grateful I am."

"First and foremost write the book you want to write, not the one you - or others - think will sell. Write with a fire in your heart and you'll create something special, something readers will want to read. There may be all sorts of received wisdom out there about 'what agents are looking for' or 'what publishers want' or 'what's selling' but who wants a second-rate copy of someone else's idea?
Write something unique to you and it will stand out from the crowd."

Jane Johnson, Editor, HarperCollins

"Writing is not for the weak or timid.
It requires courage to face the page every day.
To send out queries that may not even be answered,
to pour yourself into a story that may or may not be read,
and to lay yourself bare to a world that may only reject you."

71765099R00123

Made in the USA
Columbia, SC
05 June 2017